355.8 10-99

355.8 10-99

Brassey's *History of Uniforms*

Also from Brassey's:

Brassey's Book of Camouflage
Brassey's Book of Uniforms

Brassey's History of Uniforms

American Civil War: Confederate Army
American Civil War: Union Army
Napoleonic Wars: Wellington's Army
Napoleonic Wars: Napoleon's Army
Mexican-American War 1846-48
English Civil War
Roman Army: Wars of the Empire
Barbarian Warriors: Saxons, Vikings, Normans
Spanish-American War 1898
World War One: British Army
World War One: German Army
British Army: Zulu War to Boer War

Brassey's *History of Uniforms*

World War One British Army

By Stephen Bull

Colour plates by Christa Hook

Series editor Tim Newark

Brassey's London • Washington

In memory of E.R. Bull: Private, Artists Rifles; Lieutenant, York and Lancaster Regiment; second in command, brigade trench mortar battery; and Ministry of Munitions, 1914-18.

First English Edition 1998

UK editorial offices: Brassey's Ltd, 33 John Street, London
WC1N 2AT
UK Orders: Marston Book Services, PO Box 269, Abingdon,
OX14 4SD

North American Orders: Brassey's Inc,
PO Box 960, Herndon, VA 22070, USA

Stephen Bull has asserted his moral right to be identified as
the author of this work.

Library of Congress Cataloging in Publication Data available
British Library Cataloguing in Publication Data
A catalogue record for this book is available from the British
Library

ISBN 1 85753 270 8 Hardcover

Typeset by Hedgehog, Upton-upon-Severn, Worcestershire.

Printed in Hong Kong
under the supervision of M.R.M. Graphics Ltd,
Winslow, Buckinghamshire.

Contents

Introduction

According to the 'Official History' of the Great War the Expeditionary Force of 1914 was 'incomparably the best trained, best organised, and best equipped British Army which ever went forth to war'. This may possibly have been so, but if it was the case, then this state of training and equipment had been achieved at the expense of scale. Whilst France kept approximately 850,000 men with the colours, and the Germans were thought to have approximately 950,00 before calling on any additional manpower, the 'BEF' was, at the outset, just four divisions of infantry and one of cavalry, with a further two divisions of infantry to be formed in France by the end of August 1914. The total strength of the British army on the Western Front was initially barely 140,000. These were the comparative few who earned the Kaiser's nickname of 'contemptible little army' and bore the brunt at Mons and Le Cateau.

Not surprisingly these mainly Regular Army 'Old Contemptibles' were merely a fraction of Britain's potential armed strength, even in 1914. A similar number of regulars did duty in India, the Middle East and elsewhere in the large and far flung Empire, to which so much of the country's military resources were traditionally devoted. The regulars were backed not only by 'reservists', many of whom were immediately recalled to the colours, but by over 250,000 'Territorials'. This Territorial Force had come into existence as a result of the Secretary of State for War R.B. Haldane's reforms which came into place on 1st April 1908. The Territorials went a long way

towards creating order out of the apparent chaos and lack of a 'definite plan' which had pertained beforehand, and effectively created a single category of part time soldier out of the various Volunteer battalions, whilst the ancient Militia became a 'special reserve'. The Territorials were administered, though not commanded, by County Associations headed by the local Lord Lieutenant. Whilst a considerable advance the Territorial system had two apparent weaknesses: the first of these was that although members of the force were liable for home service they were not expected to serve abroad unless they had given their personal consent. Secondly it was initially proposed that the Territorials would not be committed to combat straight away, but, though mobilised at the outbreak of war, would then do six months training and preparation.

Regulars, Reservists and Territorials alike were all fitted into the old regimental system, by being made numbered battalions (or companies and batteries), of the Regiments and Corps, some of which dated back to the 17th century. Thus it was that the first and second battalions of most infantry regiments tended to be the regular battalions, which had originally been brought together as a result of earlier army reforms in the 1880s, whilst the third and sometimes fourth battalions were usually the Reserves and Extra Reserves. The next couple of battalions of most regiments were those of the Territorial Force. Soon after the outbreak of war the picture was further complicated not only by the rapid expansion of the Territorials but by the appearance of Service battalions, popularly known as 'Kitchener' battalions after the Victorian war hero Field Marshal Lord Kitchener who had been newly appointed as Secretary of State for War. It had been Kitchener who had immediately issued a 'call to arms' under the now famous slogan, 'Your Country Needs You', a brilliantly successful recruiting campaign which helped push the numbers volunteering to almost 300,000 in August

Opposite.

A 2 inch Trench Howitzer, or 'toffee apple bomb thrower' crew in Mesopotamia, 1917. Neck flaps have been added to the Wolseley Pattern helmets, and the corporal, left, appears to be wearing rank chevrons attached to a shirt and a spine pad. This picture also shows the wooden bed of the piece and the rifle mechanism which was used to fire the trench mortar.

IWM Q 24289

1914, and 1.2 million by the end of that year. Conscription was therefore avoided until 1916. By the end of the war over 22 per cent of the male population, or just short of 5 million, had enlisted. By that time 1.8 million of these would be on the Western Front. Another 700,000 were dead, most of them again on the Western Front, with well over 2 million having been wounded, some invalided out, and others returned to the ranks.

It may be useful at this point to show by means of an example exactly how the various Regular, Reserve, Territorial and Service battalions fitted together in practice to make up a sample regiment of the line. The Loyal North Lancashire regiment might perhaps be chosen as in many ways typical of the army as a whole in 1914. It had come into existence in 1881 as a result of the amalgamation of the 47th and 81st regiments of foot, and until the beginning of the war had just two active battalions of regulars. On 4 August 1914, the 1st Battalion was based at Tournay barracks Aldershot, and since it had been allotted to 2nd Brigade of the 1st Division of the BEF it immediately proceeded to France, disembarking at Le Havre on 13 August. It remained on the Western Front until the final Armistice over four years later. 2nd Battalion was at Bangalore, India, on the outbreak of war: in October it sailed for German East Africa, where it would serve for some time before being sent to South Africa to recuperate. It later served in Egypt, and did not reach the Western Front until June 1918. 3rd Reserve Battalion had a comfortable war by comparison, for having been embodied at Preston, it was transferred to Felixstowe area in September 1914, and here it spent the entire war as part of 'Harwich Garrison'.

The 4th 'Territorial Force' Battalion of the Loyal North Lancashire's (later known as 1/4th), was embodied at Avenham Lane Preston at the start of the war. It equipped and trained at Swindon, Sevenoaks and Bedford, with various formations, prior for departure for the Western Front in May 1915. The 5th Battalion (subsequently redesignated 1/5th), though formed at Bolton, had a similar history, training at Chipping Sodbury and Sevenoaks before entering the French theatre of war in February 1915. Such was the level of recruiting into the Territorials in the first three months of war that duplicate battalions, the 2/4th and 2/5th were quickly raised in the same home towns: these would proceed to the Western Front in early 1917. During 1915 a third echelon of Territorials was formed at Preston and Bolton, designated appropriately enough 3/4th and 3/5th Battalions 'Territorial Force'. These never served in France and Flanders, being absorbed into reserve

battalions and stationed in Ireland in 1918. Yet another Territorial battalion of the Loyal North Lancashire Regiment was the 4/5th which reached the Western Front in early 1917 and was absorbed by 1/5th Battalion in February 1918. Four final Territorial battalions raised by the regiment followed distinctly different paths; 1/12th, formed at Lytham in 1915, was designated as pioneers and served not only in France but Greece and Egypt; 2/12th was also formed at Lytham, but got no further than Oswestry before being absorbed by a reserve battalion. The 13th and 14th Battalions of the Territorial Force were the product of the reorganisation of the Home Service Territorials at Blackpool. Again these units got no further than Essex prior to disbandment. The 11th were a further Reserve Battalion.

The Loyal North Lancashire Regiment also included six 'Service' battalions, numbered as 6th, 7th, 8th, 9th, 10th and 15th battalions. All except the last were 'Kitchener' units formed in the usual way in the Preston area, but the 15th was formed at Cromer, Norfolk, and absorbed the 11th Battalion of the King's (Liverpool Regiment) later becoming pioneers in France. All the Service battalions except one would see service in France and Flanders: the 6th was in Gallipoli, Egypt and Mesopotamia.

The Loyal North Lancashire Regiment would therefore raise a total of 21 battalions during the course of the Great War, although not all of these of course were in existence simultaneously. This was by no means an unusually high number, for between them the 69 regiments of the line would raise no less than a total of 1619 battalions: an average of a little in excess of 23 battalions each. Although most regiments did ultimately have between 15 and 35 battalions, there were a few notable exceptions to the 'average' sort of performance. Recruiting in Ireland, though good, never did match that on the mainland, and was blighted not only by the 'Home Rule' question but the 1916 Rebellion, and the relative thinness of the population. The Irish regiments generally therefore tended to have fewer battalions; the Royal Irish managed just ten, the Leinster regiment only seven, and the Connaught Rangers six. The same was true of a few unusual regiments that were 'Territorial' only; the exclusive Honourable Artillery Company never had more than three battalions, the Monmouthshire's ten, the Cambridgeshire's four and the Herefordshire's three. At the other end of the scale certain units managed huge numbers of battalions, particularly in the conurbations of the south east and north west of England. The all Territorial London Regiment for example finally made an unsurpassed 88 battalions, the

King's Liverpools 49, the Royal Fusiliers 47, and the Manchesters 44 battalions.

The Guards and the cavalry, as might perhaps be expected, never fell in with the general plan of Regulars, Territorials and Service units, and in the main their regiments remained far smaller than their line infantry equivalents. The Guards regiments only raised 18 battalions between them, perhaps the most significant addition to their ranks coming in February 1915 with the formation of the Welsh Guards. Like the line the Guards also formed 'Machine Gun Companies', but unlike the line machine gun units, which would ultimately become the 'Machine Gun Corps', Guards machine gun units retained a separate identity. In 1918 was created the Guards Machine Gun Regiment, the remainder of which was created by dismounting the Household Cavalry.

Expansion of the cavalry began in 1914 with the formation of 17 Reserve Cavalry Regiments, three for the Household and 14 for the line. The Yeomanry were doubled in 1914 by the creation of a second regiment for each existing formation, and then brought to triple their pre-war strength in 1915 by the addition of a third regiment. Thus it was for example that the Royal Wiltshire Yeomanry, originally one regiment strong, formed a second regiment in 1914, and a third in 1915; these being known respectively as the 1/1st, 2/1st and 3/1st Royal Wiltshire Yeomanry. By the time these expansions were well under way it was becoming progressively more evident that mounted troops were of strictly limited usefulness in modern war. Many Yeomanry units were therefore dismounted and sent to Gallipoli, converted to cyclists, kept at home and in Ireland, or fought in the Middle East where the war remained somewhat more fluid. By 1917 this use of manpower was seen as a distinct luxury as the maw of the Western Front devoured the available troops, and a general programme of dismounting the Yeomanry to fight on foot was therefore begun. In several instances the origin of the new units so created was commemorated in lengthy titles, as was the case with 13th (Scottish Horse Yeomanry) Battalion the Black Watch; 10th (Shropshire and Cheshire Yeomanry) Battalion the King's Own Shropshire Light Infantry, or 15th (Hampshire Yeomanry) Battalion the Hampshire Regiment. A whole infantry division, the 74th (Yeomanry), was created in the middle east, and this was shipped en block to fight on the Western Front in 1918.

The 18 pdr stuck in the mud near Zillebeke, August 1917. Drag ropes, sheets of corrugated iron and shovels are used by the other ranks toiling in their shirt sleeves. Even an officer joins in trying to clear the barrel from the mud. IWM Q 6236.

Service Dress and Full Dress

On the eve of the Great War the British private soldier had two basic uniforms, Full Dress for ceremonial and state occasions, and Service Dress worn for training and active service. Which equipment and accoutrements were worn with each uniform depended on the task in hand – 'full marching order' for example entailed carrying complete equipment and pack. Additional to the basic uniforms were a variety of other garments for special purposes. Amongst these were items such as the waterproof coats issued to Army Service Corps drivers, canvas 'frocks' and trousers worn on fatigues, and the leather flying gear and 'cord pantaloons' worn by members of the infant Royal Flying Corps.

Contemporary postcard illustration showing a colour party of the York and Lancaster Regiment dipping their colours in a Royal Salute, c.1914. The uniform worn is the scarlet full dress with white regimental facings. The officers are distinguished not only by their swords and shoulder straps but by decorative lace at the collar and cuff, and waist sashes. Senior non-commissioned officers are identified by the wearing of their crimson sashes over the right shoulder, and both officers and senior non-commissioned officers wear white gloves. The spiked 'blue cloth' or Home Service helmets and the blue trousers with stripe at the seam, are in practice almost black in colour.

THE YORK & LANCASTER REGIMENT
Dipping the Colours in a Royal Salute.

Drum Major and bass drummer of the Royal Warwickshire Regiment in full dress. The Drum Major, who carries the parade staff, has wings on the shoulders of his uniform, wears gauntlet style white gloves, and both the ornamental embroidered regimental sash of the Drum Major, and the ordinary sash of the senior non-commissioned officer. The drummer's uniform is ornamented with wings and stripes of red and white on the sleeves; over this is worn the bass drummer's leopard skin.

Officer and senior non-commissioned officer of the Royal Warwickshire Regiment. The officer wears the undress double breasted Universal Pattern blue frock coat, waist sash and undress blue cloth forage cap with scarlet band and welts. The non-commissioned officer wears the full dress tunic with the blue facings appropriate to a Royal Regiment: notice the white piping, shoulder straps with regimental title, and the regimental antelope cap and collar badges.

The issue, storage, longevity and disposal of all other ranks clothing was governed by the *Regulations for Clothing of the Army*, published by the War Office in 1914, which ran to over 200 pages of minutia. These regulations specified that Standard Patterns for garments were to be deposited at the Royal Army Clothing Department, and that Sealed Patterns agreeing in all 'essential particulars' were to be sent out to units to ensure uniformity in such areas as application of badges, and unit level work carried out by Sergeant Tailors and their assistants. Contracted manufacturers were likewise guided by the officially sanctioned Sealed Pattern, deviation from this norm being good reason for the refusal of non standard or otherwise imperfect items. Most garments were supplied 'made up', but fitting for individuals and

other minor work was carried out by the unit tailors. The items of uniform 'personal clothing' on issue to a regular infantryman of the line in Britain in 1914, comprised: 'Ankle boots , black leather, two pairs; forage cap; Service Dress cap; woollen drawers; two pairs; canvas "frock" coat (for fatigue duty etc.); Service Dress jackets, two; puttees, two pairs; canvas shoes, one pair; canvas trousers; Service Dress trousers, two pairs; dress 'tweed' trousers; dress tunic; cardigan.'

It was specified that these items were all to be kept by the soldier, and maintained by him in a good state of repair with the aid of a quarterly clothing allowance which was credited with the pay. In addition each soldier was given various items of 'public clothing', maintained centrally, but designed to last set periods of time. These items when lost, damaged, *(continued p.14)*

Top.

The main guard of the 9th (Queens Royal) Lancers at Canterbury, 1911. All five non-commissioned officers and men wear the blue cloth double breasted jacket of the lancers. The regimental facing was scarlet. Though the majority of the group wear the full dress lance cap with drooping black and white plume, the bugler wears the blue cloth forage cap with regimental cap badge. The corporal wears both his rank chevrons and a regimental arm badge on his right sleeve. 9th / 12th Lancers collection, Derby Museums.

Left.

Private of the Duke of Lancaster's Own Yeomanry, 1913. The Duke of Lancaster's was one of several yeomanry regiments to boast a sumptuous dress uniform: seen here is the scarlet serge Patrol Jacket with four pleated patch pockets with gilt regimental buttons on the flaps. There are five larger but similar buttons on the front fastening, and chain mail shoulder chains. The collar badges on the plain blue collar are in the form of a Lancashire rose. The headgear is a highly polished Albert pattern helmet with white plume, brass fittings, and a plate in the form of the arms of Lancaster. DLOY Regimental Collection.

Top.

Men of the 20th Hussars on guard duty at their barracks, c.1914. The dark blue dress uniform with yellow frogging is worn with the busby, or in the case of the bugler depicted, with the forage cap. The regimental busby bag of the 20th was crimson, and the plume, when worn, yellow. Scarlet busby bags were worn by the 7th, 8th, 10th and 15th Hussars; the 4th and 14th had yellow; the 19th wore white; the 18th, blue; the 13th had buff; and a shade known as 'garter blue' was worn by the 3rd. The distinctive regimental plumes were white for the 3rd, 7th, 13th, 14th and 19th; scarlet for the 4th and 15th; red and white for the 8th; black and white for the 10th; crimson and white for the 11th; and scarlet and white for the 18th. 14th / 20th King's Hussars Regimental Collection.

Right.

Rifle Brigade officer in full dress, c.1900. One of the most distinctive pre-war full dress uniforms was that of the rifle regiments. This officer wears the rifle green tunic with black velvet collar and cuffs, decorated with five cord loops, and Austrian knots on the lower sleeve. The headgear is a black Persian lambskin busby with a plume of black ostrich feather, and the gloves are of black leather. The shoulder belt is of regimental pattern, complete with whistle and chains, and the sword is the 1827 Pattern rifle officer's with a black sword knot looped around the guard.

Hand coloured photograph depicting signallers of the Royal Horse Artillery with a heliograph, c. 1914. Hussar style braided jackets and busbies are shown teamed with overalls and boots. The inverted chevrons worn over the decorative sleeve knots are good conduct stripes, above which are the crossed flags proficiency badges of the qualified signaller. Notice the single rank chevron of the Bombardier worn on the right arm only: Royal Artillery rank nomenclature was changed in 1920 so that Bombardier would later become a two stripe rank. Under the heliograph are two signal flags.

Sergeant Northumberland Fusiliers in full dress. Distinguishing features include the Fusilier cap; flaming grenade cap and collar badges and red over white hackle. The green regimental facings to the jacket were unique amongst the Fusilier regiments: most Fusilier regiments included the word Royal in their title and were thus entitled to blue facings, whilst the facings of the Lancashire Fusiliers were white.

or prematurely worn out, had to be paid for separately by the soldier. These pieces were, in the case of the line infantryman, the great coat and blue cloth helmet, both of which had a specified life span of five years. Interestingly the Guards bearskins, the busby of the hussars and horse artillery, lance caps and other pieces of uniform for mounted regiments were expected to last even longer. The headgear which was intended to last longest of all was the highland feather bonnet which had a predicted life of no less than 12 years.

Wolseley pattern helmets and certain other items were only issued for stations abroad. At the time of issue the marking of clothing entrusted to individual soldiers was carried out. These markings were applied inside the clothes and were officially in three parts, the

initials of the unit being stamped above the man's regimental number, which in turn appeared above the month and year of issue. Thus it was that according to the letter of the rules, a Service Dress jacket issued to 1418 Private Smith of the Royal Irish Regiment in April 1902 should have been marked 'R.I.R.', over '1418', over '4/02'. Needless to say such meticulous stamping was not always adhered to, especially after the outbreak of war.

For officers, matters were rather different, as they received an allowance, and, rather than having uniforms issued, were given the addresses of regimentally approved tailors and instructed to have their own kit made up. The rules which applied to officers' dress were not to be found in *Clothing Regulations*, but in *Dress Regulations* which were also issued periodically in printed form. The 1900, 1904 and 1911 editions of the officers *Dress Regulations* and

Piper and bandsmen of the Highland Light Infantry. The piper wears the traditional kilt with green doublet, but the bandsmen wear tartan trews, scarlet doublets with yellow facings, and the unusual regimental green cloth 'Chaco' with green ball tuft and diced band.

Other ranks of the Army Service Corps pictured in both Full Dress and Service Dress, c.1908.

the 1913 updates not only described garments, lace, swords and badges, but in many cases provided photographs and diagrams. The South Lancashire regiment collection still has a small framed display which contains samples of cloth with War Office seals showing the types of material from which officers' dress was to be cut, and a sample tie and collar which were supposed to act as guides for these privately ordered garments.

As might be expected, officer's uniforms were generally of superior quality and cut, and included certain pieces, like Mess Dress jackets, which were not worn by other ranks. Officers were also able to adopt 'undress' for occasions more formal than actual field service, but not requiring the whole panoply of 'full dress'. Such instances might include courts of inquiry, or courts martial, boards, and afternoon dances and receptions.

Full dress for other ranks and for most practical purposes came to an end in August 1914: most of it

was 'baled' and stored away until the cessation of hostilities, and issues to most units ceased. Exotica like the busby, fusilier cap, lance cap, blue cloth 'Home Service' helmet, and parade ground scarlets disappeared virtually overnight. Full dress would survive after the war essentially only in the Household Cavalry and Guards, bands, and for officers appearing at levees and at a few ceremonial events.

Field uniforms and clothing designed with concealment in mind had been around for many years by the time the First World War broke out. 'Rifle' and 'Jäger' green, brown, and even black uniforms dated back to the 18th century with many armies. In the British instance not only the regular Rifle Corps but many of the volunteers had taken to dull hues during the course of the 19th century: the Rifle Volunteers of the 1860s in particular had adopted not only the familiar rifle green, but a number of shades of grey for their companies. In India there had been early and regular use of various types of lightweight clothing, including garments made of drab Khaki cotton coloured with various vegetable dyes, including, so it is said, tea and coffee. The word 'khaki' was itself

Top left

A young bugler of the Gloucestershire Regiment in Service Dress c. 1914. Notice the regimental sphinx cap badge and the lanyard worn around the left shoulder.

Above.

A suave looking private of the Essex Regiment, his Service Dress being set off with a lanyard, cane, watch fob, and long service good conduct chevrons.

Left.

An atmospheric studio portrait of a private of the Bedfordshire Regiment, showing clearly the star, Maltese cross and Hart cap badge, and the brass Bedford shoulder title.

derived from the Urdu for 'dusty'. For the Second Ashanti War of 1873 Major General Sir Garnet Wolseley ordered grey uniforms for campaign, an experiment which was expanded upon during the Egyptian Expedition of 1881-82. Here British, and British Indian, forces would appear not only in scarlet and khaki but in grey serge.

Further home trials during the later 1880s produced an 'invisible grey' uniform, an experimental khaki frock coat, and some extraordinary garments in brown corduroy. None of these were ever accepted as

Highland Service Dress as worn in a studio portrait by a sergeant of the 2/9th (Highlanders) Territorial battalion of the Royal Scots, April 1916. In addition to the Glengarry headdress, kilt and leather sporran, the Highland version of the simplified war time Service Dress is worn with rounded skirt fronts to the jacket. Note both the Imperial Service badge on the right breast and the 1914 Pattern leather belt with its distinctive snake clasp. The 'Dandy Ninth' were unusual in that they were a kilted battalion in a regiment which mainly wore 'S.D. trousers'.

Sergeant piper James Stoddard and his sons, Liverpool Scottish, 1914. Amongst the distinguishing features of the uniform are dress sporrans, ornate belts, and a *Skean Dhu,* literally translated as a 'black knife' pushed down the hose, over which are worn khaki gaiters. The tartan worn by the unit was the Forbes sett. Note also the manner in which the drummer wears the greatcoat rolled over the shoulder.
Liverpool Scottish.

a 'universal' standard but they certainly helped to change the climate of opinion, and showed the potential of the use of colours less obvious than red. It was also during this decade that the problems associated with non fast khaki dye were solved by chemist Frederick Gatty who patented a mineral dye of this colour in 1884. Within ten years non fugitive 'khaki drill' was being worn as a matter of course by British troops in India and Africa, and by 1896 it was being worn on all foreign stations. Khaki cotton drill uniforms were worn in South Africa during the Boer war, and from 1900 these were supplemented by khaki serge.

The khaki serge Service Dress in which the Great War would be fought had thus been in gestation for many years under various guises, but had only finally been introduced in a universal form for all troops by Army Order in January 1902. It was described as 'designed with a view to furnishing a comfortable uniform, light enough to be worn on service abroad, and in warm weather at home, and also with the addition of warm underclothing, for winter wear at home'. The cloth was to weigh between 18 and 20 ounces per yard, and was of a drab khaki woollen mixture.

By 1914, other ranks' Service Dress comprised a flat topped khaki cap with peak, badge and thin brown leather chin strap; single breasted khaki serge jacket; and matching leg wear. In most units this leg wear was trousers worn with puttees (the name 'puttee' coming from the Hindustani for 'bandages'), but for mounted men breeches were teamed with the puttees or gaiters.

In the infantry the puttees were generally tied at the top; in the cavalry, at the ankle. The Service Dress jacket was distinguished by a stand and fall collar, five brass General Service buttons, cloth reinforcements over the shoulder area and shoulder straps. Rifle battalions wore black, or blackened, buttons. In practice most units wore brass shoulder titles on the shoulder strap but there were certain exceptions, including some Guards battalions which wore cloth titles at the top of the sleeve. There were four pockets to the jacket, the breast patch pockets originally having box pleats. In most instances the jacket was supplied by the manufacturer with a paper label inside the wearer's right hand side, on which were recorded

Left.
Detail of other ranks' Service Dress jacket, 1915, showing the pleated breast pocket, shoulder reinforce, shoulder strap, General Service buttons, and collar which was closed with hooks and eyes.

Below.
Interior detail of the unlined Service Dress jacket showing the maker's label and white taping reinforcement. This particular garment was made by S. Sneiders and son, 1915: it is to fit a small man five feet four inches in height with a 35 inch chest.
Queen's Lancashire Regiment.

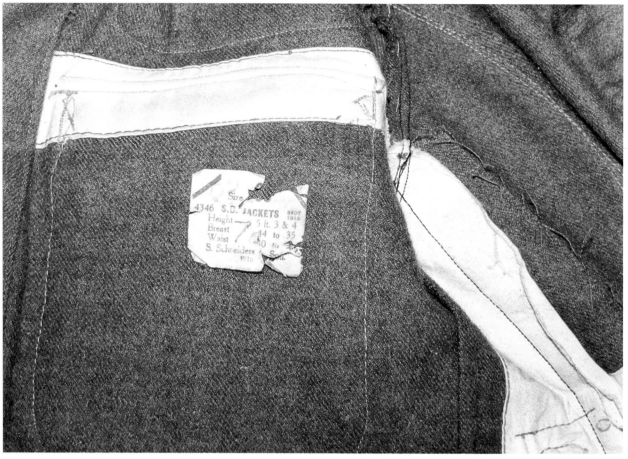

not only the maker's details, but the size fitting and the date. The jacket was not lined, but certain internal seams were reinforced with a white, or off white, tape.

The Service Dress trousers were generously fitting and, though there were no belt loops, could be worn with either a belt or braces. Underneath were worn loose drawers, photographic evidence on which demonstrates the wearing of both long and shorter 'boxer' legged varieties. Perhaps surprisingly one Imperial War Museum series of photos shows Highlanders of a Black Watch Battalion wearing the boxer short variety at a sporting event. They are of baggy white cotton, and reach about half way down the thigh.

Scottish units that wore the kilt had rounded skirt fronts to the jacket, and although popular literature has since described this garment as a doublet it was always officially described at the time as a jacket, Highland Pattern, or Scottish Regiments. The kilts themselves were of varying regimental tartans, the natures of which are summarised at the end of this section: but at the front, although Service type plain leather sporrans were not unknown, the majority of Highlanders wore no hairy purse and covered the tartan cloth by means of the issue kilt apron. This apron of plain khaki cloth was a skirt-like garment, secured at the waist, which not only protected the kilt but improved camouflage. Kilts were worn with hose and gaiters, or spats. Opinion varied as to the suitability of Highland dress to warfare: the kilt had a splendid appearance and was a substantial piece of warm pleated cloth, but whilst it offered considerable freedom of movement and circulation around the crotch, there were distinct drawbacks in mud. The folds of the cloth could also harbour vermin, and even when clean and dry, highland costume weighed more than the standard jacket and trousers.

Highland and certain Lowland Scottish units were further marked out by the wearing of the Glengarry headgear. According to regulation there was not one, but several slightly varying versions of this 'fore and aft' folding cap. For most regiments it was dark blue, plain for the Black Watch and Cameron Highlanders, but with a diced band around the edge for the Seaforths, Gordons and Argyll and Sutherland Highlanders. All these had a scarlet tuft. The Cameronians, as befitted a rifle regiment, had dark green Glengarrys with a tuft of similar hue; whilst the Highland Light Infantry, so often an exception, wore the dark green Glengarry but with a diced band. Territorial Highland units raised within England similarly wore Highland garb including the Glengarry, that of the Liverpool Scottish for example being of the blue type with dicing.

It does appear, however, that the exigencies of service soon began to blur some of the niceties, and in any case the Glengarry was not found to be entirely practical, and was quite rapidly supplemented by a round beret-like Scottish cap, known as the Balmoral bonnet. This hat was relatively small and close fitting, and was sometimes seen with a khaki field cover. Later in the war both the Balmoral and the Glengarry gave way to a large drab Tam O' Shanter: the 'T. O.S'. was by contrast fairly loosely fitting, and maintained a reasonable degree of practicality whilst being distinctive. Another advantage was that it was sufficiently voluminous and malleable to accommodate the large badges which were general with other forms of Highland service head dress.

Captain Albert Ball V.C. in the officers' Service Dress of the R.F.C.: a portrait in oils by Noel Denholm Davis (1876-1950). The celebrated air ace is depicted in the khaki drab Service Dress jacket with shoulder mounted rank badges, metal R.F.C. collar titles, pilots wings and medal ribbons. Also shown are the light coloured breeches and Sam Browne belt. Many flying officers preferred to wear the Service Dress of their old regiments with the addition of relevant badges. Nottingham Castle Museum.

A studio portrait of a private of the Liverpool Scottish, 10th (Territorial) Battalion The King's Liverpool Regiment, c. 1914. He wears the Glengarry with diced border, regimental badge and ribbons; Service Dress jacket with cut away front of 'Highland Pattern' and shoulder titles denoting battalion and regiment; kilt of Forbes tartan with dress sporran and regimental horse of Hanover motif; spats and hose. Liverpool Scottish.

A portrait of a Scottish soldier and friend taken in an Edinburgh studio showing the cut away Highland or Scottish regiments S.D. jacket being worn with trousers.

Regimental Tartans

Few subjects are as vexed in the history of military dress as Scottish tartans, there being disputes even as to the derivation and meaning of basic descriptive terms. Yet it can be said with some confidence that many of the patterns or 'setts' in use in the army in 1914 were descended originally from the Government cloths of the mid and late 18th century, commonly associated with the Black Watch, in which greens, blues and black predominated. Others types introduced into the service context later in the 19th century boasted various family, royal and clan connections. The 'Hodden' or 'Elcho' grey used by the Territorial London Scottish was not a tartan in the popular sense at all, for it lacked any check or pattern, yet this plain coloured material also had a

distinguished military past since it had not only family connections with Lord Elcho, but had been the traditional coat colour of Scottish regiments as long ago as the 17th century.

In regular Highland units the regimental tartan was of course most commonly seen in the kilt of all ranks, though, as has been noted, at the front on active service it was usually covered by a khaki drill apron. Even in regiments which did not wear the kilt, or had Lowland antecedents, tartan had its place since 'Trews' of tartan cloth were often worn by officers when Service Dress trousers were worn by the rank and file. According to the 1911 *Dress Regulations* Trews were permissible in full, undress and mess dress for officers in Highland regiments; the Royal Scots; Royal Scots Fusiliers; King's Own Scottish Borderers; Scottish Rifles (Cameronians); and the Highland Light Infantry. Photographic evidence suggests that Scottish officers, even in the same regiment on the same service, might wear different legwear. Tartan Pantaloons, rather like breeches, were also authorised for mounted duty.

Above.
Service Dress as worn by other ranks of the Royal Flying
Corps. Until 1918 and the creation of the RAF, the Flying Corps
was regarded as a corps of the army. Note the wrap over style
Service Dress jackets and cloth shoulder titles. The man
holding the hare wears a winged observers badge just above
the right elbow.

Top Right.
Officer cadet John 'Jack' Todd, Royal Flying Corps, 1917. Todd
wears the officer quality R.F.C. Service Dress with voluminous
breeches, side cap with distinctive officer trainee white cap
band, and a private purchase identity bracelet. He was killed in
a flying accident in July 1918 whilst serving with the RAF.
Lancashire Museums.

Right.
A portrait of a painfully young looking private of the Royal
Flying Corps. He wears the Service Dress of the corps with
cloth 'Royal Flying' over 'Corps' shoulder titles and side cap.
Notice how the buttons of the jacket are concealed. D.D.

Even where a whole regiment with Scottish
connections was wearing khaki on active service it was
still usual to maintain kilted pipers. In some cases the
pipers were themselves entitled to a special tartan not

Private, Northumberland Fusiliers, 1916.

The central figure represents a private soldier of the 16th (Service) Battalion (Newcastle), Northumberland Fusiliers, 1916. Raised by the Newcastle and Gateshead Chamber of Commerce in September 1914, the Newcastle 'Commercials' were landed in France just over a year later. On 1 July 1916, they were committed to the opening of the attack on the Somme as part of the 32nd (New Army) Division effort against the Thiepval sector. They were led to expect little resistance, but even as they formed up the enemy started to pick them off with rifle fire, then began gesturing and goading them on.

The attacking companies of the 'Commercials' then advanced 'like one man', without wavering, but as the battalion War Diary records, the leading waves were rapidly chopped down by rifles and machine guns. A bugler, still standing in the trench beside the Commanding Officer heard him exclaim 'My men, my men, my God my men !', and saw that he had to be physically prevented from clambering out over the top after them. The Colonel then ordered that the remainder of the battalion man their front line fire step, returning fire without attempting any further advance. After nightfall the stretcher bearers found 'in several places, straight lines of ten or twelve dead or badly wounded, as if the platoons had just been dressed for parade'. The unit was later reinforced, and continued to fight on the Western Front, but was eventually disbanded in February 1918.

The Newcastle Commercial depicted here wears the standard Service Dress, with the Pattern 1914 leather equipment. A steel helmet would have been worn during the actual assault, but he is shown here in the Service Dress cap complete with Northumberland Fusiliers regimental cap badge. Other distinguishing features include the 'NF' and flaming grenade brass shoulder titles, and the red triangle over red bar battalion battle insignia at the top of the left sleeve. His weapon is the Short Magazine Lee Enfield .303 inch rifle, fitted with both 1907 Pattern bayonet, and the wire cutter which had been approved in 1912 and was produced in quantity by several manufacturers during 1916.

Down the left hand side are shown the constituent parts of the Pattern 1908 web infantry equipment. At the top is the belt with bayonet, frog and entrenching tool helve, and the haversack. Just below are the water bottle and the entrenching tool head in their carriers. The main pack is shown stowed with a steel helmet in a sacking cover, which has been splotched with camouflage paint in a style seen in photographs of 1917. The ammunition carriers came in left and right sets of five, to contain a total of 150 rounds. The left hand carrier is of the type with modified fastenings.

At the bottom of the illustration appears a ten pocket 'waistcoat' grenade carrier of a type in use from 1916 onwards, complete with a 'No 5' Mills grenade. At the bottom right of the picture are seen two Yukon heavy load packs of the type in service during the last two years of the war. One example is empty, the other is stowed with water cans. The steel helmet, centre right, bears the red elephant motif of the 10th Battalion Duke of Wellington's regiment.

The selection of five regimental cap badges are the tiger and rose of the York and Lancasters; the dragon of the Buffs; the Britannia of the Norfolks; the Sphinx of the Lincolnshires; and the bugle horn of the Duke of Cornwall's Light Infantry. The detail top right is the text book method of fastening the 1908 web belt. *Painting by Christa Hook.*

common to the unit as a whole. There was also at least one 'English' unit, the University and Public Schools battalion of the Middlesex Regiment, which had kilted pipers. The situation was further complicated not only by the distinctions of territorial units, both Scottish and English, but by the fact that there were certain regiments that had some battalions which wore Service Dress trousers, and some which wore the kilt. This was the case with the Highland Light Infantry where just the 6th and 9th battalions were kilted; and the Royal Scots in which only the Edinburgh 'dandy' 9th Battalion was so attired. In the cases of the London, Liverpool and Tyneside Scottish, these were Scottish Territorial and New Army battalions within a larger English Regiment which itself did not wear highland dress. In summary, the major regimental tartans worn by the army during the Great War were as follows:

The Royal Scots	Hunting Stuart (only 9th battalion kilted)
The Royal Scots Fusiliers	Black Watch or 'Government' pattern (regiment not kilted)
The King's Own Scottish Borders	Leslie (regiment not kilted)
The Cameronians (Scottish Rifles)	Douglas (regiment not kilted)
The Black Watch	Black Watch (pipers Royal Stuart)
Highland Light Infantry	Mackenzie (only 6th and 9th battalions kilted)

A Lieutenant of the 20th Hussars, c. 1916. Notice not only the Service Dress jacket but the shirt and tie worn with tie pin, and the 'XHX' ('XX'-20th; 'H'-Hussars) cap and collar badges. The rank badges are worn on the shoulder straps. 14th / 20th King's Hussars collection.

A portrait of an elderly but dapper Royal Army Medical Corps officer, May 1916. The open collared Service Dress is here worn with Sam Browne, cravat, breeches, leggings, spurs and a neck flap or trench version of the Service Dress cap. The three rank pips of a captain appear on the sleeve of the jacket: these jackets with cuff rank insignia are sometimes referred to as 1908 Pattern.

Seaforth Highlanders	Mackenzie (or Ross-Shire Military) 5th Battalion 'Sutherland'
Gordon Highlanders	Gordon
Cameron Highlanders	Cameron (Cameron of Erracht)
Argyll and Sutherland Highlanders	Black Watch
Tyneside Scottish	Black Watch (not kilted but units wore Scottish headgear and Black Watch tartan badge backing) Pipers only 'Hounds Tooth' or Shepherd's Pattern black and white kilts. This unit was

originally part of the Northumberland Fusiliers

| Liverpool Scottish | Forbes, part of King's (Liverpool Regiment) |
| London Scottish. | Hodden or 'Elcho' grey, part of the London Regiment |

The Royal Flying Corps

Apart from the Highlanders, the only other unit to have an instantly recognisable form of Service Dress of their own was the Royal Flying Corps, which had been founded in 1912 and was until the last year of the war treated as a Corps of the army. Perhaps because

Textbook officer's Service Dress as worn by a subaltern of the Army Service Corps, c. 1915.

Regimental Sergeant Major of the 14th (King's) Hussars, c. 1918. The Service Dress worn is of officer quality with Sam Browne, but unlike the officer's uniform is closed to the neck. The jacket is worn with breeches, laced at the knee, and leggings. Rank badges and overseas service chevrons are worn on the sleeves: the cap badge is the Royal crest within a garter which temporarily replaced the more familiar Prussian 'Hawk' badge of the regiment. 14th / 20th King's Hussars collection.

the aircraft was regarded as a 'mount', and because the early duties of the Corps in reconnaissance were similar to those of light cavalry, certain peculiarities of style in attire were adopted from the lancers. The most important of these was the plastron front to the jacket which buttoned right across, the buttons themselves being concealed both on the jacket front and on the shoulder straps. What looked elegant on a horseman in full dress could, however, appear ungainly in khaki serge, and the RFC Service Dress soon earned itself the sobriquet 'maternity jacket'. It was generally worn with a two part cloth shoulder title with the words 'Royal Flying' over 'Corps'. According to one account the original design work on the RFC jacket was aided by the long established firm of Gieves, the naval and military outfitters which would later go on to provide vast amounts of uniforms for RAF officers.

RFC officers could, and often did, wear the Service Dress uniform of the regiment from which they originated instead of the new wrap over jacket: flying 'wings' were sanctioned for wear on the breast during the war, as was the 'O' with a single wing which

denoted observers. Photographic evidence suggests that prior to being used on the chest, small observer badges were positioned on the right arm by other ranks in the same way as other army proficiency badges. Blue-grey uniforms were only introduced in 1918 with the formation of the RAF, but even then they were regarded as optional, being worn sometimes as a type of mess dress.

Officers' Service Dress

Officers' Service Dress for all other units was readily identified not only by better quality materials but certain details of style. The *Dress Regulations* of 1911 discussed the original officers jacket at some length , describing it as: 'drab mixture serge; to be of the same

Field Marshal Sir Douglas Haig and his senior generals pictured at Cambrai on Armistice Day, 1918. Most wear a Service Dress of near regulation type for this semi formal group photograph, but even here variations are apparent. Both Haig and Rawlinson, the commander of 4th Army, omit the shoulder strap to the Sam Browne: both carry canes but the much decorated Rawlinson wears a cravat rather than a tie. Shirts vary considerably in shade; the elderly Plumer, commander of 2nd Army, shown front left, wears a shirt of unfashionably dark khaki. Horne, the commander of 1st Army seen on the right, wears the more formal peaked forage cap complete with gold braid or 'scrambled egg' whilst many others wear Service Dress caps with or without stiffeners.
IWM Q 9689.

colour as that issued to the men; single breasted; cut as a lounge coat to the waist , very loose at the chest and shoulders, but fitted at the waist; . . . military skirt . . . a hook on each side at the waist; jacket cut low in front of the neck; turn down (Prussian) collar, to fasten with one hook and eye.' The breast pockets of the jacket were pleated and sewn down at the top corners so that on active service they could be opened up to provide a larger capacity.

Some of these 'closed collar' five button jackets survived until the war and some were worn at the Front, yet by 1 August 1913 a new plate and an amendment had been issued to be added to the *Dress Regulations* showing a new style Service Dress jacket for officers with the now familiar open collar and lapels, and only four regimental buttons down the front, to be worn with a drab flannel shirt and tie. To the late 20th century eye, the jacket had an especially long skirt (actually supposed to measure 13 inches for an officer of 5 feet 9 inches height); it was also equipped with voluminous side pockets, and the pleated breast pockets. Inside the jacket was normally to be found a watch pocket, as described in the regulations, complete with a leather tab to which a pocket watch chain could be attached. This detail would survive some time, even though a wrist watch was actually specified for both mounted and dismounted officers, and many indeed soon found the watch worn on the wrist far more convenient as it could easily be used even when carrying a weapon, or blowing a whistle to signal the attack. The officer's S.D. jacket was further distinguished by collar badges, or 'dogs', not generally possessed by the rank and file in most regiments. These were to be worn above the 'step' in the collar or lapel. Highland officers wore a special version of the Service Dress jacket cut away at the

Three different variations on the other ranks great coat. The Lance Corporal postman, with the impressive leather post bag, is a member of the 1/4th (Hallamshire) Territorial Battalion of the Duke of Wellington's regiment and wears the single breasted dismounted pattern coat. The other dismounted pattern coat is worn by a rather shell shocked looking member of the Royal Fusiliers: his coat lacks the shoulder reinforces, but does show the tab which buttons across the coat to close it at the throat. The third man, of the Machine Gun Corps, wears the shorter double breasted mounted pattern coat.

front, and with a gauntlet style cuff, agreeing in general configuration to the Service Dress of other ranks in Highland units. Regulation allowed officers' jackets of all types to be either lined or unlined, but in most instances it appears that lined jackets were actually chosen.

The tie that was supposed to be worn with all officers' Service Dress was to agree to a Sealed Pattern, be drab in colour and tied in 'a sailor's knot': according to the letter of the law tie pins were not to be worn . In the event the rules regarding ties seem to have been honoured more in the breach than the observance; and officers appear to have worn around their necks either whatever they could get away with, or whatever the commanding officer of their unit deemed appropriate. Photographic evidence from

the war years therefore shows not only neat drab ties but broad 'kippers' of widely varying tone, tie pins and ornaments. Rakish cravats also made an appearance especially in the less formally regulated Corps, and a particularly splendid example was frequently sported by no less an officer than General Rawlinson.

Strictly speaking the mounted officers' nether wear was limited to Bedford Cord breeches laced at the knee, of the same hue as those worn by other ranks. Surviving examples and contemporary literature again suggest a more catholic approach was taken in practice; sometimes the colour of the whipcord breeches was described as beige, and more often than not they buttoned rather than laced at, or rather slightly below, the knee. Knickerbocker breeches of a drab serge mixture similar to the trousers of non commissioned officers and men were to be worn by dismounted officers. Breeches could be worn with puttees, gaiters, brown ankle boots, 'butcher boots', or long 'field boots'. The 1911 regulations specified brown leggings of Stohwasser pattern for all mounted officers, but by 1913 amendments stated that riders who did not wear the 'field boot' would wear a brown leather legging, agreeing to a Sealed Pattern, which closed up the front by means of laces and six studs.

Both Officers and other ranks wore a great coat over the Service Dress in cold weather, with a longer single breasted model for dismounted men and a shorter double breasted version for mounted troops. Officers' great coats were described as of Universal Pattern: 'Cloth, drab mixture, milled and water-proofed; double breasted, to reach within a foot of the ground; stand and fall collar. . . fastening with two hooks and eyes; cloth tab and buttons; a 2 1/2 inch inverted expanding pleat down the centre of the back . . . two rows of buttons, four in each row . . . lined on shoulder and sleeve only.'

Regulations also speak of Arm of Service coloured edges to the shoulder strap of the officers' great coat but how far this feature was actually applied is not clear. Optional officers' waterproofs were also allowed, in Atholl Grey for senior officers, and khaki drab mixture for others. These were intended to be of a single breasted Inverness style, having five bone buttons to the body and a cape style top fastened with a further four buttons. Sealed Patterns were apparently produced but even the *Dress Regulations* acknowledged that these were only to govern general appearance. In the event it appears that the Inverness Waterproof was not very widely worn.

Portrait of an army chaplain, dated 1916. He wears Service Dress over clerical collar and civilian waistcoat; the officer's trench cap is of the type with folding neck flap and strap. Clearly visible are shoulder pips denoting his rank of captain, possibly on coloured 1902 type shoulder straps, and cap and collar badges showing a cross surmounted by an Imperial crown common to the various Christian denominations.

Decorations and Identity Tags

According to regulations, short lengths of medal ribbon were to be worn with Service Dress and were mounted on the left breast of the jacket, over the pocket, in a specified order of precedence. This system of precedence, as laid down in August 1912, put the Victoria Cross first, followed by the various Orders (including the Distinguished Service Order), followed by the Jubilee, Coronation and Durbar medals. Next in line were the Distinguished Conduct Medal, campaign medals, life saving, police, long service and others. Last in precedence were any awards bestowed by foreign countries: these were worn with official permission only, and in the event the Great War foreign medals most often granted were the French and Belgian Croix de Guerre. In some instances, as with the 1914 Star, the medal was formulated and the

Youthful and probably under age Kitchener volunteers outside their bell tent, c. 1914; the pair on the left wear a tolerably standard version of the dark blue 'emergency' uniform, with side cap. The proud character on the right has received a khaki Service Dress jacket and forage cap, but no badges.

The blue emergency uniform as worn by two men of 8th (Service) Battalion the King's Own, 1914. Notice the circular battalion badges worn on the collar in lieu of anything more regulation. King's Own collection, Lancaster City Museum.

ribbons issued as the war continued; but with the well known Service and Victory medals these obviously had to wait until after 1918. Photographic evidence supports the common sense conclusion that the campaign ribbons most frequently seen being worn by serving troops in 1914 were those of the King's and Queen's South Africa medal.

Worn under the Service Dress were the man's identity tags, usually a pair, in dull green and red fibre respectively, suspended from the neck on string. Normally the men wore and preserved them without prompting, for without them their fate might remain unknown to their relatives, especially if they were parted from jacket and pay book. Some men indeed doubled up on the official provision by wearing an unofficial metal wrist bracelet with their name. Strictly speaking burial parties were instructed to remove one of the two official tags, leaving the other with the body which was to be buried with due ceremony in an issue white body bag. Locally made wooden crosses were supplied as soon as possible, being replaced only after the war by the War Graves Commission by the now familiar regimentally decorated head stones. In practice things were seldom so organised. Bodies often went unrecovered, or were mutilated without tags. Official bags were replaced by blankets, or even sand bags: and the better chaplains who stuck with their flocks at moments of crisis rightly spent more time ministering to the living, or to the dying, than to the dead. In a quiet sector, at base hospital, or for an airman who fell behind the line, full military honours might be respected; during a 'big push' it was almost certain to be otherwise.

'Kitchener Blue' and 'Hospital Blue'

In theory, the above remarks would have been pretty much all that could be said about the Service Dress and its embellishments, were it not for the huge wave of new recruits, shortages and exigencies of service, which soon led to quite significant changes and

A surprisingly happy looking Corporal Thomas Bradshaw and two friends in captivity near Hanover, Germany, August 1917. All three wear dark blue uniforms whilst the man on the right retains the cap badge of the Sherwood Foresters, Nottinghamshire and Derbyshire Regiment.

British soldiers in German captivity wearing dark blue uniforms with tan coloured inserts, designed to render them more conspicuous in the event of an escape attempt. Close examination of the photograph reveals strips of the telltale material up the legs of the trousers, incorporated into the band of the cap, and in a band around the upper left arm, as is the case in the surviving Imperial War Museum uniform.

variations. To start with, supplies of issue Service Dress rapidly dried up and many recruits, especially in 'New Army' battalions, had no uniform at all in the early days of training and were frequently to be seen drilling in civilian costume, complete with cloth caps, bowlers, straw boaters, shirts and ties. A few at least got lapel badges to show their military affiliation: 14th, 15th and 16th Battalions of the Royal Warwickshires, for example, had a badge with the Royal 'GR' monogram over 'Birmingham Battalion 1914'. The University and Public Schools Brigade had a badge with the intertwined initials 'U.P.S.'

As an interim measure, many men throughout the 'New Armies' were issued with what was officially called Emergency Pattern dark blue serge Service Dress, also known as the 'Kitchener uniform', or derogatively as 'workhouse blues', often complete with a matching side cap. Some Kitchener men even received blue greatcoats. As new Service Dress became available the blue uniforms were replaced, but it was

by no means unusual to see new recruits in a mixture of dress. Though the Imperial War Museum collection includes a Sealed Pattern Emergency blue Service Dress photographic evidence suggests that there was actually quite wide variations in what was worn. Some uniforms have large breast pockets with buttons, others none at all: likewise some had shoulder straps and some not. One authority suggests that some of the earliest blue uniforms actually came from the Post Office.

There were equally wide differences in the regimental distinctions applied to Kitchener uniforms. Some units wore it without any regimental badge at all, others put on badges, arm bands, shoulder titles and collar badges with little reference to any published regulation. It is known for example that certain battalions of the Suffolk and Northamptonshire regiments wore regimental shoulder titles attached to their collars: 8th Battalion of the King's Own Royal Lancasters wore a circular white ceramic collar badge with the inscription '8 K.O.R.'; 12th (Service) Battalion of the West Yorkshire Regiment adopted a narrow arm band, worn on the left upper arm, with the legend '12. W.Y.'. Some of the York and Lancaster's also sported an arm band which appears to have taken the form of a strip of cloth with a badge in the centre. 8th (Service) Battalion of the Loyal North Lancashire regiment had an oblong badge sewn to the left upper arm on which appeared '8th BN' over 'LNL'.

Dark blue uniforms were also supplied to Germany, where they were worn by British prisoners in enemy captivity. An example of the British prisoner's uniform in the Imperial War Museum has a section cut out of the left sleeve, and replaced with brown cloth. Removal of this identifying strip would have left the would be escapee lacking one sleeve. A similar strip of brown cloth was apparently also inserted down the trouser seam, and sometimes even around the band of the peaked cap. Photographic evidence also shows prisoner of war blue uniforms without the brown cloth inserts and with a variety of collar types, suggesting perhaps the re-use of obsolete jackets. Convalescent officer prisoners, and probably others, were also given a loose fitting striped pyjama suit. This was given a modicum of smartness by officers who wore it with shirt and tie.

Another type of blue uniform, considerably lighter in colour than the 'Kitchener blue' and cheaper to produce, was used for the thousands of men who became casualties, and was worn in the hospitals and convalescent homes of Britain. Again there appears to have been significant variation: in one form the jacket terminated at waist level, in another there were skirts to the thigh. Lapels also varied, being often the same colour as the main body of the jacket, but sometimes of a lighter shade. 'Hospital blue' was particularly useful for it not only marked out men who had 'done their bit', and gave them a comfortable and practical outfit, but it also helped medical staff identify charges who had strayed off limits. Like the prisoner's uniform the hospital outfit was often worn with a cap with the man's regimental cap badge. The tie was red.

Although various shades of blue predominated amongst the Emergency Service Dress, prisoner and hospital uniforms, other colours were occasionally

British POWs of several different regiments, showing the full gamut of prisoner clothing, blue, blue with brown inserts and Service Dress. Note that in this instance a camp number in Roman numerals and a personal number in Arabic numerals have been sewn to the left breast.

encountered. It is known that certain new Kitchener battalions adopted grey, brown and even green striped with grey prior to the issue of regulation khaki. Perhaps the best examples of this practice were the units of the Welsh Army Corps, much of which was later committed to action as 38th Welsh Division. In addition to khaki and blue uniforms the Welsh also received suits of Brethyn Llwyd, or Welsh grey 'homespun' which could vary considerably in shade, the contracts for which seem primarily to have been handled by various Cardiff firms. At least 8,000 suits of Brethyn Llwyd were finally supplied, made by more than a dozen Welsh woollen mills primarily in the southwest of Wales. This was in spite of the fact that it was considerably more expensive, for whilst a Service Dress jacket of blue cost just 14s 2d, a few pence less than the 14s 7d paid for 'proper' khaki, a jacket of Brethyn Llywd cost a pound.

Outside the Welsh Army Corps units there were also other battalions with temporary uniforms of strange shades. 11th (Service) Battalion the Welsh

A group portrait, c. 1916, showing men of different Scottish and English regiments fresh from the front. Several men wear cut off shorts, the corporal of the Gordons, right, wears the Tam o' Shanter and two wound bars on the left cuff of his jacket.

Regiment, which was not Welsh Army Corps, nor supplied by the Welsh National Executive Committee, contracted privately with Jotham's outfitters of Cardiff for its own version of Brethyn Llwyd. The result was a uniform a little browner in colour than khaki and gained the unit its 'Chocolate Soldiers' nickname. There were also at least a few English units initially clad in grey, such as 11th (Service) Battalion of the Border regiment.

Regimental cap badges would remain a particular problem for a long time: some new battalions adopted special designs of their own, but there were also a variety of temporary expedients in use. One was the use of simplified discs: a good example of this practice was the 11th Battalion of the Welsh Regiment who wore a temporary badge with the words 'The Welsh Regiment' in the centre, and 'Cardiff Commercial Battalion' around the outside. The 6th Battalion of the South Wales Borderers adopted a tin badge with the abbreviation '6 S.W.B.' and this was sometimes worn on the collar rather than the cap. More widespread was the use of a General Service button instead of the cap badge; and photographic evidence suggests that this practice occurred in a majority rather than a minority of regiments. To allow production to catch up, most of the standard badges were also simplified, usually by substituting an all brass model where

previously a bi-metal badge had been worn. Although strictly speaking General Service buttons bearing the Royal Arms should have been worn by the infantry with Service Dress, it does appear that some battalions ignored the rule and used regimental buttons.

Badges were a particular problem for prisoners of war in Germany, and many men never did solve this difficulty and were seen wearing their blue prisoner outfit without regimental emblems. Others, who were lucky enough to have retained their existing badges on capture, were able to transfer them to their new costume. The most resourceful however were those who made new badges in captivity. In the museum of the Royal Warwickshires are a number of examples of rather rough looking insignia, both cap and rank badges, which were fabricated by heating up small pieces of scrap metal with low melting points, and recasting them in the desired shape.

Even when the troops had complete Service Dress and were ready to proceed abroad there were still variations. In many New Army units the local dignatories who had helped to raise the battalions had not waited to receive official supplies of clothing but had immediately contracted for their manufacture with whatever company could undertake to deliver. This had the advantage not only of sidestepping the

Kitchener Volunteers muster on a park c. 1914. The photograph has been artfully posed so that the minimal amount of equipment available is on show. This unit appears to have just one stretcher, and five obsolete guns, of which one seems to be a shot gun. Although several men have puttees, Service Dress is limited to two officers and one man's jacket, again strategically positioned near the camera.

official government contractors, who already had more orders than they could complete, but it put work in the hands of local men who were often supporters of the recruiting effort. Some units scratched and scraped with obsolete patterns of uniform, others sometimes even received temporary issues of full dress, but with some expense was no object and they went straight for the best. 22nd Battalion Royal Fusiliers, for example, took their order directly to the managing director of Harrods department store who supplied them with some of the last khaki available in London. The same unit purchased khaki shirts, rather than regulation grey, direct from Derry and Toms, and leather equipments from Lillywhites, which at that time was better known for its cricket gear. It was therefore no wonder that there were variations both in the cut and colour of Service Dress and in accoutrements.

A private of the Middlesex Regiment, c. 1916, and lady friend. He is wearing a simplified or 'economy' version of the Service Dress; this lacks the pleats in the breast pockets of the jacket as well as the shoulder reinforcement panels.

A wounded sergeant of the Essex Regiment, c. 1917. The 'hospital blue' is worn open at the neck with shirt and tie. The short jacket is fastened with five buttons and has the rank chevrons applied to the right sleeve only: coloured bands, which might perhaps identify the hospital, are worn around the cuffs. The cap has bands of stitching around the peak and bears the regimental badge.

Very soon alterations were also being made deliberately, both with a view to simplification of manufacture and to practicality. Pleated pockets and shoulder reinforcements for example quickly disappeared as a matter of expediency, though later in the war they would be reintroduced. Soldiers at the front, especially in the summer of 1916, also took to cutting down their trousers to make shorts: this must have become relatively commonplace since it was eventually forbidden by a *General Routine Order* issued that October.

As as been widely observed, once they were at the front the peaked Service Dress caps often had their wire stiffeners removed, making them a less obvious shape to the enemy observer. An official variation to the Service Dress cap came in the winter of 1914, with the introduction of a soft model with a neck flap and ear flap which could be slipped under the chin, or when not in use fastened over the crown of the head. Though widely seen especially during 1915 and 1916 it never became universal, and both types of cap

coexisted. Photographic evidence and surviving dated examples show that in the last two years of war most Service Dress caps appear to have been made without stiffening, of lighter weight material, with lines of stitching reinforcing the peak and band, and a black water resistant oil cloth interior. They have been popularly christened 'Trench caps'.

There were also changes wrought by shortages and matters of practicality in the attire of the Highlanders. The simplification of the headgear has already been touched on but there were also other alterations. Some units, expanding rapidly, ran out of regimental tartans and at least a few equipped men in patterns which were technically speaking incorrect. Photographic evidence shows that some Highland battalions, particularly later on in the war, abandoned the kilt, at least temporarily, and wore Service Dress trousers or even shorts in their stead. Many other pictures show highland troops wearing not spats or gaiters but half length puttees with knee length hose or socks.

Territorial units not only suffered shortages and employed variations in dress, but also possessed, and often maintained, a number of distinctions some of which went back to before the war. The most obvious of these perhaps was the small letter 'T', which appeared on the shoulder titles, usually over the Battalion number. Thus it was for example that 5th (City of London) Battalion, the London Regiment, wore a brass 'T' over '5' over 'City of London'. Sometimes the battalion numeral was omitted, and so it is that many surviving photographs show a 'T' worn directly over the regimental title. Another distinction frequently touted by the Territorials was the white metal badge worn on the breast which showed they had volunteered for overseas service. This was a simple oblong design, bearing the words 'Imperial Service' over which was a King's crown.

Officers' Service Dress underwent something of a metamorphosis under the pressures of war. Some officers took to the other ranks Service Dress jacket, or altered the officers' jacket to look more like the costume of other ranks – the origin of the so called 'wind up' jackets; but in most instances the effort to blend in to avoid the attention of snipers was more subtle. The most important single modification to officers' dress was perhaps the migration of rank distinctions from the cuffs to the shoulders where indeed they were already worn by Guards officers: the wearing of puttees with trousers, soft caps, 'trench boots' and other minor changes, or less than regulation methods of wear, were also commonplace. One form of headgear for officers which rapidly gained popularity was a 'trench cap' with a neck flap. When the flap was folded up, its retaining strap came to rest over the peak, lying over the leather chin strap, or replacing it entirely. Officers also wore a wide variety of alternatives to the standard greatcoat. One particular favourite was the 'British Warm', usually a double breasted coat in khaki or brown wool, shorter than the greatcoat and with leather buttons. This cost between £3 and £5 even in 1915. Macintoshes were also frequently seen, and the popular styles of the war years gave birth to the original of the 'trench coat' which has been a fashion classic ever since. Many were worn with fleece linings, particularly in winter. Numerous tailors and commercial manufacturers supplied trench coats although Burberry's received

Convalescent officers in German captivity, September 1917. They wear distinctive striped suits combined with a wide variety of private purchase shirts and ties.

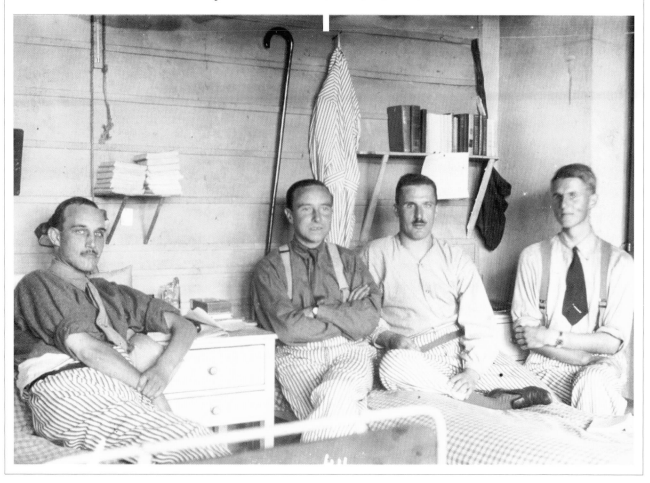

An informal moment on the beach at Ilfracombe for convalescent soldiers, summer 1915. Caps with regimental badges are worn with two slightly differing versions of a short 'hospital blue' jacket and matching trousers.

A Territorial of the Royal Army Medical Corps in Service Dress, 1914. Note the obsolete dress belt, Imperial Service volunteer badge on the right breast, and the medical orderlies' red Geneva crosses on the upper arms.

perhaps more custom and comment than any other: some officers swore by them, though one at least pronounced them 'too leaky'.

The statistics surrounding the total supply of clothing to the British forces in 1914-18 are such as to beggar belief. Amongst the many different issues were 122 million 'socks, worsted'; 36 million ankle boots, with a further 4 million supplied to allied powers; 29 million Service Dress jackets and trousers; and over 17 million cardigans and sweaters. Into shirts alone had gone 200 million yards of flannel, or enough material to go almost five times around the earth.

Above.

Royal Engineers outside the regimental tailor's workshop, 1918. The Regimental Sergeant Major, front left, is distinguished not only by his Royal Arms rank badge on the sleeve, Sam Browne belt, cane and gloves but the superior quality and cut of his Service Dress which has officer style hip pockets and pointed cuffs. The sergeant, foreground right, has the cross hatched version of the chevrons over which is worn the regulation RE flaming grenade. The other men show both the pleated pocket, and plain pocket, versions of Service Dress.

Top right.

A portrait of an Army Service Corps private, c. 1917, in the simplified Service Dress jacket, which in this instance lacks shoulder titles as well as pleats and reinforcements. The Service Dress cap is of the trench cap type current late in the war, without stiffener and with rows of stitching around the peak which would allow it to be easily stowed whilst a steel helmet was in use. The brown leather chin strap is being worn behind the 'ASC' cap badge.

Right.

Private Bill Atkinson of the 1/4th (Territorial Force) Battalion the Loyal North Lancashire Regiment, c. 1915, wearing the padded winter Service Dress cap introduced in late 1914.

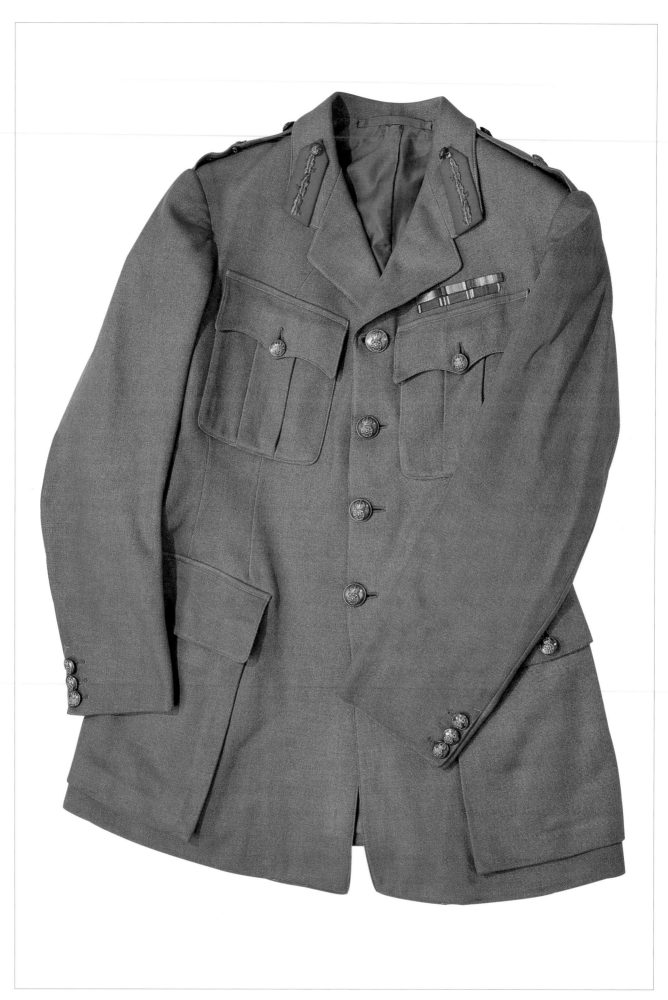

Badges and Insignia

The addition of many new badges, over and above the old regimental cap and shoulder titles and badges of rank, was a significant feature of Service Dress, especially from 1916 onwards. Certain other ranks' proficiency badges had existed long before the war: these included the crossed flags of the signaller; the hammer and pincers of the armourer and fitter; the horse shoe of the farrier; the drummer's drum, and the wheel badge of the wheeler. The war would bring with it others, many of them associated with new weapons or skills, like the grenades of the bombers and trench mortar crews, or the Lewis gunner's distinctive insignia.

Even more noticeable was the proliferation of colourful arm bands, divisional signs, wound badges and service chevrons. Arm bands were adopted not only for other ranks on specific duties, like stretcher bearers and medics, but also by various categories of officer serving with headquarters and staffs. So much did arm bands multiply that from 1915 General Headquarters was prompted to step in and attempt to regulate their numbers and design. A comprehensive table of those officially sanctioned was published with the extracts of *Routine Orders* in January 1917. Overseas service badges in the form of small chevrons worn point upwards on the right cuff made their appearance late in the war, and were awarded for each year of foreign service. The standard chevron was blue, but one in red was given to 'Old Contemptibles' who had served in 1914. The larger good conduct chevrons had existed before war, and were still worn during the conflict, but these appeared, point upward, on the left cuff. Wound badges for wear on the Service Dress jacket by all officers and soldiers who had been wounded in any campaign since 4th August 1914 were

officially sanctioned in late 1916, the authority for each award being inclusion in casualty lists. These badges or 'stripes' were to consist of two inches of gold 'Russia braid No 1' sewn perpendicularly on the left sleeve of the jacket, one for each occasion wounded. Officers were to wear the first such badge immediately above the point of the cuff flap (where they had one), whilst other ranks were to wear them three inches from the bottom of the sleeve. In both cases further

Pocket and lapel close up of the same jacket. Note the detail of the gorget patch and the top three medal ribbons which are those of the 1914-15 Star; the War Service medal and the Victory medal.

Opposite.
A staff officer's Service Dress jacket, c.1918, complete with scarlet gorget patches or red 'tabs'. The jacket is lined and has had Great War medal ribbons added post war. DLOY collection

such badges were to be added at a half inch gap. Accidental or self inflicted wounds were specifically debarred from entitlement to wound badges.

By 1916, a number of distinctly temporary markers had appeared for wear on the back during major attacks which would allow easy identification of friendly troops when viewed from the rear. Clearly seen in contemporary film were the small reflective triangular pieces of metal worn in the middle of the soldiers backs during the assault on the Somme. Captain Hitchcock of the Leinsters records the wearing of a 'white metal' disc in the same way, in the same sector, during the latter part of August 1916, but these were rapidly discarded by the men.

Probably the most impressive of all the war time badges were the colourful systems of battalion identifications and divisional signs which came into use in some units in late 1915, and in most the following year. The whole subject was remarkably complex, and intentionally so, since one of the major reasons for introducing such things in these forms was security: even today certain details for some of the schemes remain obscure. Amongst the first little signs to make their appearance however were a number of badges which were unique to an individual battalion but did not yet serve any purpose in terms of higher formations. Interesting examples included the small red, white and blue rosette sported on the side of the Service Dress cap by 8th Battalion of the South Lancashires, and the shamrock bearing the inscription '5 CR' which denoted the 5th Battalion of the Connaught Rangers current during 1915 and 1916.

Soon afterwards many divisions adopted a sign which was not only carried on vehicles and command posts but was worn by the soldier in the form of a coloured patch, usually in cloth on the upper arm of the jacket but sometimes also painted on steel helmets, or sewn to the back of the Service dress. In some instances the divisional sign was not worn by the infantry, but only by support troops. In others it featured on the command posts, whilst the men wore brigade and battalion identifiers only. The form of the divisional signs was often a play on the divisional number or an allusion to a geographical area. Thus it was for example that 'ATN' was the sign for 18th Division, for when said quickly it sounded similar to the number. 21st Division had a three legged device, each limb of which appeared like a '7', making '21' in all. 30th Division used the 'Eagle and Child' crest of the Earl of Derby, and 31st Division used red and white roses, red for Lancashire and white for Yorkshire. 12th Division, for reasons that are obscure, chose the ace of spades. 51st (Highland) Division made little

attempt at security by simply taking a large 'H.D.'

Many divisions adopted, in addition to their basic sign, a series of coloured bars, crosses, triangles, diamonds, squares and even Roman numerals worn on uniform to identify a particular battalion within the brigades of the division. One excellent example, a detailed record of which survives, was the system chosen by 4th (Regular) Division in June 1916, just prior to the Somme offensive. The Divisional sign for all units was the ram's head, a pun on the commanding officer's name which was Lambton: in addition a regimental flash was worn on the shoulder of the Service Dress. The actual brigade and battalion distinctions were worn as cloth badges sewn to the sacking covers of the steel helmet. The brigades were colour coded, and the battalions identified by the shape of their coloured patch. 10th Brigade wore green badges, 11th Brigade yellow and 12th Brigade red. In 10th Brigade the 1st Battalion Royal Warwicks

Opposite.

A pre-war photograph showing a proud military badge collector with his fine but eclectic assemblage of cap and collar badges, shoulder titles, and buttons arranged around a Home Service helmet plate. Just some of the many unit symbols represented are –

Top right quarter: **the rearing White Horse of the Queens Own (Royal West Kent Regiment); the Staffordshire Knot and Prince of Wales feathers of the Prince of Wales's (North Staffordshire Regiment); the strung bugle, crown and initials of the Durham Light Infantry; the cross and laurel wreath of the Rifle Brigade; the acorn of the Cheshire Regiment; the double headed eagle of the 1st (King's) Dragoon Guards; and the crossed lances of the 9th (Queen's Royal) Lancers.**

Bottom Right: **The antelope of the Royal Warwickshire Regiment; the dragon of the Buffs (East Kent Regiment); the star of the Order of the Thistle and bugle horn of the Highland Light Infantry; the stag's head of the Gordon Highlanders; the sphinx, rose and laurel leaves of the East Lancashire regiment; the star and castle of the Devonshire regiment; and the castle and key in a laurel wreath of the Northamptonshire Regiment.**

Bottom left: **The tiger of the Leicestershire Regiment; the Prince of Wales plumes, coronet and laurel wreath of the Duke of Cambridge's Own (Middlesex Regiment); the white horse of Hanover of the King's (Liverpool Regiment); the flaming grenade of the Royal Fusiliers, and the 'XHX' of the 20th Hussars.**

Top left: **The Roussillon plume and Garter Star of the Royal Sussex Regiment; the Royal Artillery field gun; the sphinx and laurels of the Gloucestershire Regiment; the Royal Crest, scroll and Lancashire rose of the Loyal North Lancashire Regiment; the castle and flag of the 6th (Inniskilling) Dragoons; and the black Prussian eagle of the 14th (King's) Hussars.**

A selection of divisional signs from an interwar series of cigarette cards. From top left, the eye of the Guards Division; the yellow circle and cross of 3rd (Regular) Division; the circle of 6th (Regular) Division; the thistle of 9th (Scottish) Division; the shamrock of 16th (Irish) Division; the 'ATN' of 18th (Eastern) Division; the black cross and red spot of 20th (Light) Division; the 'three sevens' of 21st Division (New Army); the red shoulder strap bar of 28th Division which fought at Salonika; and the Derby crest of 30th Division (New Army).

thus had a green horizontal bar; the 2nd Seaforth Highlanders a green vertical bar; the 1st Royal Irish Fusiliers a green square; and the 2nd Royal Dublin Fusiliers a green diamond. For 11th Brigade the 1st Somerset Light Infantry had the horizontal bar in yellow; the 1st East Lancashires a yellow vertical bar; the 1st Hampshires a yellow square; just to confuse matters, the 1st Battalion of the Rifle Brigade had a yellow Rifle Brigade cross. In 12th Brigade, 1st Battalion of the King's Own had a red horizontal bar; 2nd Battalion Lancashire Fusiliers a vertical red bar; 2nd Battalion of the Duke of Wellington's a red square; and 2nd Battalion of the Essex regiment a red diamond.

This was just one unique method amongst many. 11th (Northern) Division, whose Divisional sign of a red circle over a red triangle resembled a key hole,

used a totally different arrangement. They wore a series of coloured rectangles on the back of the collar of the Service Dress, red for 32nd Brigade, green for the 33rd, and yellow for the 34th. The individual battalions within the brigades were then identified by Roman numerals on the patch. Yet another possibility was illustrated by the case of 20th (Light) Division whose basic Divisional sign was a black cross with a red dot in the centre, all on a white circular ground. In this scheme the 'battle patches' were all black, as befitted a formation which contained a number of rifle battalions. The various brigades were then distinguished by a disc, triangle or square, under which the Battalion was signified by between one and four narrow cloth bars.

The 34th (New Army) Division, whose basic sign was a chequer board, was one of several formations whose use of divisional and battalion identifiers appears to have changed with time. Initially the division was made up primarily from the Tyneside Scottish and Tyneside Irish of the Northumberland Fusiliers, the various Scottish battalions of which were marked out by coloured diamonds worn at the back of each shoulder. In May 1918, heavy losses resulted in the division being reduced to a cadre. Nevertheless it promptly reformed, using a catholic selection of

Also from the same series, the 'four eights' of 32nd Division (New Army); the double three domino of 33rd Division (New Army); the red hand representing 36th (Ulster) Division; the golden horse shoe of 37th Division (New Army) which had been depicted inverted until late 1916; the red and white diamond of 42nd (East Lancashire) Division; the 'HD' of 51st (Highland) Division; the red rose of 55th (West Lancashire) Division with five leaves on each side; the red sword or dagger of 56th (London) Division; the yellow crosses of 59th (North Midland) Division; and the broken spur of the 74th (Yeomanry) Division.

Territorials and Regulars from both Scotland and England, including units as diverse as pioneers drawn from the Somerset Light Infantry, two battalions of the Cheshires, and a battalion of the Argyll and Sutherland Highlanders. Photographic evidence suggests that late in the war the divisional sign of a chequer board was worn on the shoulder, and that coloured rectangles were now sometimes worn on the upper arm as battalion marks.

The enemy hopefully remained in ignorance of much of this heraldic minutiae and in this way, in the short term at least, secrecy was maintained whilst brigade and divisional commanders could easily distinguish their own troops. Divisional signs also gave the men some bigger sense of formation and purpose outside their immediate regimental 'family'. It should be observed that not all of the army was adorned like popinjays all of the time: few signs were worn before 1916, and they were not commonly seen in Britain since the primary purpose of such devices was to distinguish different commands during the attack.

Ranks and rank distinctions

OFFICERS:

Field Marshal: Cap badge, crossed batons within a laurel wreath surmounted by a crown and lion.
Shoulder strap, as above but without lion. Also scarlet gorget patches with gold oak leaves, and scarlet cap band.

General: Cap badge, crossed sabre and baton within a laurel wreath surmounted by crown and lion.
Shoulder strap, crossed sabre and baton surmounted by a pip and crown. Also scarlet gorget patches with gold oak leaves, and scarlet cap band.

A group including various mounted troops: the lance corporal on the right wears the 'horse's bit' proficiency badge of the saddler, in this instance on the left upper arm.

Young Territorials of Alexandra, Princess of Wales's Own (Yorkshire Regiment) c. 1917. The man on the left wears Lewis Gunner proficiency badges in brass on both sleeves, and a bomber's badge in brass on the right shoulder.

Lieutenant General: Cap badge, crossed sabre and baton within a laurel wreath surmounted by crown and lion.
Shoulder strap, crossed sabre and baton surmounted by a crown. Also scarlet gorget patches with gold oak leaves, and scarlet cap band.

Major General: Cap badge, crossed sabre and baton within a laurel wreath surmounted by crown and lion.
Shoulder strap, crossed sabre and baton surmounted by a pip. Also scarlet gorget patches with gold oak leaves and scarlet cap band.

Brigadier: Cap badge, crossed sabre and baton within a laurel wreath surmounted by a crown and lion.
Shoulder strap, crossed sabre and

baton. Also scarlet gorget patches with gold oak leaves and scarlet cap band.

Colonel: Cuff, four rows of lace, two pips and a crown. Holders of staff appointments wore the pips and crown on the shoulder strap, and also scarlet gorget patches with a 'gimp' or chain decoration, scarlet cap band and crown and lion cap badge.

Lieutenant Colonel: Cuff, three rows of lace, pip and crown.

Major: Cuff, three rows of lace and a crown.
Captain: Cuff, two rows of lace and three pips.

Lieutenant: Cuff, one row of lace and two pips.

A private soldier wearing both the crossed rifles of the marksman, and the Lewis gunner 'LG' in brass on the left sleeve.

Second Lieutenant: Cuff, one row of lace and one pip.

N.B. Officers of the Guards regiments wore their 'Order of the Garter' rank pips and crowns on the shoulder throughout the war, and Scots Guards and Irish Guards were distinguished by Thistle and St. Patrick variations on the usual rank pip. Scottish regiments wore a gauntlet style cuff with their cuff rank badges horizontally under the rows of lace. During the course of the war the cuff rank distinctions were progressively abandoned by most officers for being attractive to sniper fire and time consuming to produce. Stars and crowns were seen more and more on the shoulder strap, and the practice was officially sanctioned in 1917. The cuff rank system was formally abolished in 1921.

Warrant and non commissioned officers

First Class Staff Sergeant Major, Conductor Army Ordnance Corps, and from 1915 Warrant Officers

A somewhat bizarre studio group of Lewis Gunners and Snipers of the Queen's (Royal West Surrey Regiment) posing with cuddly toys c. 1918. Brass Lewis Gunner proficiency badges are worn on the lower left sleeves, the fleur-de-lis of the scout or sniper is shown on the right shoulder.

1st Class: Crown within wreath on lower sleeve, (in 1918 altered to Royal Arms within wreath).

Quarter Master Sergeant (from 1918): Crown within wreath.

Other Warrant Officers, and from 1915 Warrant Officers 2nd Class: Crown on lower sleeve.

Household Cavalry Quartermaster Corporal-Majors, Quartermaster Sergeants, Saddler Corporals, and equivalents: Four chevrons.

Troop, Battery, or Company Sergeant Major and equivalents: Crown over three chevrons.

Sergeant, Lance Sergeant, and Household Cavalry 'Corporals of Horse': Three chevrons.
Corporal, and Guards Lance Corporal: Two chevrons.

Lance Corporal; Bombardier: One chevron. Standard chevron lace was a woven buff, or white, and drab worsted, but some regiments retained a regimental pattern lace. Royal Artillery NCOs above the rank of corporal wore a gun badge above their rank distinctions. Royal Engineer and Guards NCOs above the rank of corporal wore a small grenade badge above the chevrons. In most cavalry and yeomanry regiments NCOs ranking as corporals and above were entitled to a special regimental arm badge, worn either above or occasionally on, the chevrons on the right arm. Interesting examples include the French eagle of the Scots Greys; the Irish Harp of the 5th Lancers and 8th Hussars; the skull and crossbones of the 17th Lancers; the Prussian eagle of the 14th Hussars; the ducal coronet of the Duke of Lancaster's Own; the Prince of Wales feathers of the East Riding Yeomanry, and the leek of the Welsh horse.

Orders of dress other than Service Dress sometimes entailed the wearing of badges not given above. Full details are contained in the official *Clothing Regulations* of 1914; the *Dress Regulations*, and Major P. Dawnay's *The Badges of Warrant and Non Commissioned Rank in the British Army*, Society For Army Historical Research, Special Publication number 6, London 1949.

Arm Bands (as authorised in *Extracts from Routine Orders*, January 1917).

Arm Band	Left or right arm	Worn by
Red over blue	R	General Headquarters
Red, black, red	R	Army HQ
Red, white, red	R	Army Corps HQ
Light blue with red stripe lengthwise across centre, dark blue edging and lettering 'R.F.C.'	R	R.F.C. HQ
Red, 'C.D.' in black letters	R	Cavalry Division HQ
Red	R	Divisional HQ
Blue, 'C.B.' in black letters	R	Cavalry Brigade HQ
Blue	R	Infantry Brigade HQ
Red, with embroidered gun and 'C.D.' in black	R	Cavalry Divisional Artillery HQ
Red with embroidered gun	R	Divisional Artillery HQ
Dark blue, 'G.H.Q. Trps' in red letters	R	G.H.Q. Troops HQ
Red, 'L of C' in black letters	R	Lines of Communication
Black, with 'P.M.' in red letters	R	Provost Marshal
Black, with 'A.P.M.' in red letters	R	Assistant Provost Marshal
White over blue	Either	Signal Service
Black, 'M.P.' in red letters	R	Military Police
White, 'R.T.O.' in black letters	R	Railway Transport Officer
White, 'Embark' in black letters	R	Embarkation staff
White with blue anchor	R	Inland Water Transport
Yellow	Either	Servants to Military Attachés
White, 'S.B'. in red letters	R	Stretcher Bearers
White, with red cross	L	All Medical Personnel
Green	Either	Press Correspondents and Servants
Red, 'T.C.O.' in black letters	R	Train Conducting Officers
Brown canvas 'Train Conductor' in black letters	R	Train conductors
White, 'Checker' in back letters	R	Checkers
Black, 'Town Major' in red letters	R	Town Majors
Black, with 'Traffic' in red letters	R	Traffic control
Lilac with 'A.P.S.' in black letters	R	Special Constable recruited from reoccupied territories
Yellow, with or without crossed machine guns	R	MG Schools Instructors, MGC base depot
Blue with embroidered gun	R	Heavy Artillery Corps HQ
Red, White and Green vertical stripes	R	'Special Brigade' (R.E. Gas Troops)
Green, with 'Cadet School' in silver lettering	R	Cadets in school
Green over black	Not specified	Divisional Gas Officer

Officers were instructed to wear HQ and staff arm bands only at Headquarters, and at this date the wearing of numbers to indicate formation was discontinued. Flags for HQ cars followed the colours of the arm bands, except that the Union flag was supposed to be reserved for the Commander in Chief. In addition to the above there are also known to have been others in use, both official and unofficial, and certain bands were introduced between 1917 and the end of the war. Perhaps the most important of these was the Tank Corps armlet, at first blue with red edges and an embroidered white tank, later with horizontal bands of green, red and brown. There are also in existence at least a limited number of divisional 'staff' arm bands,

in scarlet, upon which appear a divisional sign.

A number of 1 1/2 inch wide bands to be worn on the left forearm were also authorised for use in the latter part of the war, intended specifically to 'assist liaison and organisation after an attack'. According to *The Training and Employment of Divisions* of January 1918, these were:

Green band	Scouts
Red band	Runners
Blue band	Regimental and Company signallers
Yellow band	Carrying parties
Khaki band with 'Salvage' in red	Salvage parties

Proficiency badges worn on service dress

Description	Position on arm	Meaning
Crossed rifles (and variations)	Lower left	Marksman, also instructors
Crossed hammer and pincers	Upper right	Armourer, fitter, or similar
Horses bit	Upper right	Saddler, harness maker
Horse shoe	Upper right	Farrier or shoe smith
Wheel	Upper right	Wheeler
Spur	Upper right	Riding instructor
Crossed Axes	Upper right	Pioneer
Crossed flags	Lower left	Signaller
Crossed swords	Upper right	Gymnastics instructor
Crossed swords	Lower left	Best swordsman
Crossed Lances	Lower left	Best with lance
Red cross in circle	Upper, either	Medical orderly
Fleur-de-Lys (or 'S' in wreath)	Upper right	Scout or sniper
'L' in wreath	Upper right	Gun layer
Cannons crossed	Lower left	Battery prize winners
'G' in wreath	Lower left	Prize winning gunner
Whip, or whips, and spur	Lower left	Skill in driving
Diamond, or five pointed star	Lower right	Volunteers efficiency
'MG' in wreath	Lower, either	Machine gunner
'LG' in wreath	Lower, either	Lewis gunner
'HG' in wreath	Lower, either	Hotchkiss gunner
'O' in wreath	Upper right	Observer
'O' with wing	Upper right, or breast	Observer, RFC
Red, or brass, flaming grenade	Upper right	Bomber
Grenade, white flames	Upper right	Bombing officer
Blue grenade	Upper right	Trench mortarman
'QI' in wreath	Lower left	Instructor, field engineering
'R' in wreath	Lower left	Range taker
Drum	Upper right	Drummer
Lyre	Various	Bandsman
Tank in white	Upper right	Trained tank crew

Service Head Dress Badges

Service dress caps were a general issue at the outbreak of war, and continued to be worn behind, and often in the line, even after the introduction of the steel helmet. Highland units eventually replaced their Glengarrys with Tam O'Shanters, and these too continued in general use when the helmet was not required. The distinctive badge of these head dresses was often the only easy way to distinguish one unit from another, especially when shoulder titles were obscured or not worn. Many regiments had long established badges, numbers or symbols which had only to be adjusted in scale to fit the new 'S.D.' caps. Most of these, as far as they related to the officers of the regular army, were described in the *Dress Regulations* of 1911.

Other cap badges were relatively new innovations: the design worn by the Life Guards for example had been adopted as recently as 1913, and was actually issued in 1914. The 14th (King's) Hussars found their Prussian Eagle or 'Hawk', proudly borne since the 18th century, a distinct liability and changed it during

Regimental Military Police wearing the arm band 'R.M.P.' on either cuff, c. 1917, contrary to the strict letter of the regulations then pertaining.

the course of the war. The Welsh Guards and the new Corps similarly needed new badges; and some Service battalions came up with symbols entirely different to that of their parent regiment. The Territorial London Regiment was always a minefield so far as cap badges was concerned, and got worse after 1914. A number of territorial battalions in various regiments bore 'South Africa' battle honours on their badges, or where appropriate omitted such distinctions, or adopted other variations. Also noticeable during the course of the war were simplifications in manufacture and economy measures, which led to the introduction of many all brass badges where previously bi-metal, gilding metal and white metal had been used. Colour changes have been omitted from the following summary, as have the Yeomanry, Reserve, Volunteer Force and Cadet badges.

The following list is intended as a useful aid, but cannot pretend to be exhaustive as some units employed a number of types, and often minor differences for officers' badges as well. Some of the Emergency measures adopted are noted in the section on Service Dress, but readers who wish a more comprehensive treatment of this complex subject would be well advised to consult A.L. Kipling and H.L. King *Head Dress Badges of the British Army*, vol. one, (revised edition, London, 1978). Note that

abbreviated unit titles have been used here for reasons of space: full titles will be found in the section listing the regiments and corps.

Household Cavalry

1st Life Guards	Royal cypher within a circlet inscribed 'First Life Guards', surmounted by Imperial crown.
2nd Life Guards	Royal cypher within a circlet inscribed 'Second Life Guards', surmounted by Imperial crown.
Royal Horse Guards	Royal cypher within a circlet inscribed 'Royal Horse Guards', surmounted by Imperial crown.
Household Cavalry	Royal cypher within garter, surmounted by Imperial crown.

Cavalry

1st Dragoon Guards	Double headed Austrian Eagle over a scroll inscribed 'King's Dragoon Guards'. Replaced by a star and 'KDG' in 1915.
2nd Dragoon Guards	The word 'Bays' in gothic lettering, within a laurel wreath surmounted by a crown.
3rd Dragoon Guards	Prince of Wales plumes, coronet and motto on a scroll inscribed '3rd Dragoon Guards'.
4th Dragoon Guards	Star of the Order of St. Patrick, with a scroll inscribed '4th Royal Irish D. Guards'.
5th Dragoon Guards	White horse of Hanover between 'V' and 'DG', within a circlet inscribed 'Vestigia nulla retrorsum', surmounted by a crown.
6th Dragoon Guards	'VI' over 'DG' within a garter surmounted by a crown, on a background of crossed carbines. All over a scroll inscribed 'Carabiniers'.
7th Dragoon Guards	Demi lion and coronet crest of

	the Earl of Ligonier, on a scroll inscribed '7th Dragoon Guards'.
1st Dragoons	Crown with Royal crest on a scroll inscribed 'The Royal Dragoons'.
2nd Dragoons	French style eagle with a laurel wreath around its neck, standing on a tablet inscribed 'Waterloo'. Below, a scroll inscribed 'Royal Scots Greys'.
3rd Hussars	White Horse of Hanover above a scroll inscribed '3rd King's Own Hussars'.
4th Hussars	Circlet inscribed 'Queen's Own Hussars' with spray of laurel and

An interesting selection of badges worn by a private of the Liverpool Scottish, 1918. The regimental head dress badge is worn on the Tam O'Shanter, and regimental shoulder titles are visible. On the left sleeve are both a wound stripe, and, near the top, the red rose of Lancashire sign of 55th Division.
Liverpool Scottish.

Two Service Dress caps. The officer's example, which carries a blackened badge of the South Lancashire Regiment, is equipped with a neck flap. The other ranks trench cap carries the crossed machine guns badge of the Machine Gun Corps, is dated 1918, and is internally lined with water resistant oil cloth. The narrow strap is of brown leather, secured by two very small General Service buttons. Visible on the peak and band are rows of small stitching, commonly a feature of late war manufacture caps. G.C./ M.S.

	numeral 'IV' in the centre, surmounted by a crown.	8th Hussars	Irish Harp surmounted by a crown, on a scroll inscribed '8th King's Royal Irish Hussars'.
5th Lancers	Circlet inscribed 'Quis Separabit' with a spray of laurel, with the numeral '5' in the centre, all on crossed lances.	9th Lancers	Numeral '9' surmounted by a crown on crossed lances, across the lances a scroll inscribed 'Lancers'.
6th Dragoons	Inniskilling Castle flying the flag of St. George, above a scroll inscribed 'Inniskilling'.	10th Hussars	Prince of Wales plumes, coronet and motto on a scroll inscribed '10th Royal Hussars'.
		11th Hussars	Crest of Prince Albert with a scroll below inscribed 'Treu und Fest'.
7th Hussars	Monogram 'QO' within a circlet inscribed '7th Queen's Own Hussars' surmounted by a crown.	12th Lancers	Prince of Wales plumes, coronet and motto on crossed lances; numeral 'XII'.
		13th Hussars	Numeral 'XIII' within a circlet inscribed 'Viret in Aeternum', all within a laurel wreath surmounted with a crown, on a scroll inscribed 'Hussars'.

14th Hussars	Prussian eagle discontinued in 1915 to be replaced by a Royal crest within a garter, with a scroll.	19th Hussars	Crowned cross (Danish 'Dannebrog') and 'A'.
15th Hussars	Royal crest within a garter, resting on 'XV.KH.', above a scroll inscribed 'Merebimur'.	20th Hussars	The numerals and letter 'XHX' surmounted by a crown.
16th Lancers	Crossed lances with the number '16' surmounted by a crown, and a scroll inscribed 'The Queen's Lancers'.	21st Lancers	Crossed lances on which is a 'VRI' cypher with a crown above and 'XXI' below.

Guards

17th Lancers	Skull and cross bones, with the words 'Or Glory' on a scroll.
---	---	---	---
		Grenadier Guards	Flaming grenade with or without Royal cyphers.
18th Hussars	The number '18' over an 'H' within a circlet inscribed 'Pro Patria Conamur'. Surrounded by a laurel wreath, surmounted by a crown, two small scrolls reading 'Peninsula' and 'Waterloo'. Also variations.	Coldstream Guards	Order of the Garter star.
		Scots Guards	The star of the Order of the Thistle: showing St. Andrews cross and a thistle.

A private soldier of the South Wales Borderers, c. 1917, in a somewhat eccentrically modelled trench cap, wearing the crossed flags of the signaller on his left sleeve.

A study of a Royal Army Medical Corps private showing very clearly both the detail of the Service Dress, and the cloth red on white Geneva cross which signified a medical orderly. The device is outlined in bullion on a black ground. Photographic evidence shows the badge being worn on one or both upper arms.

Irish Guards	The star of the Order of St. Patrick, the design of which incorporates a circlet with the motto 'Quis separabit', the numerals MDCCLXXXIII, and a shamrock.		Birmingham Pals battalions (14th, 15th and 16th battalions) wore a similar emblem but with the addition of a scroll reading 1st, 2nd or 3rd 'Birmingham Battalion'.
Welsh Guards	A leek.	Royal Fusiliers	Flaming grenade on which is the Garter and a rose: the form of the flames more upright than that of the Grenadier Guards or Northumberlands. 25th battalion had a '25' on the ball of the grenade and a scroll with a variety of possible inscriptions which included the word 'Frontiersmen'. The Jewish battalions (38th, 39th, 40th and 42nd) wore the seven branched candle stick of that faith, with a scroll inscribed in Hebrew 'Kadimah'.
Guards MG Regiment	Garter with cypher of King George V, surmounted by a crown, on crossed machine guns, with a scroll reading 'Guards M.G. Regiment'. Also a different badge with a star formed from five bullets, the monogram MGR and the motto 'Quinque juncta in uno 1916'.		
Infantry			
Royal Scots	A star of the Order of the Thistle, on which is a figure of St. Andrew, and a scroll with the inscription 'The Royal Scots'.	King's Liverpool	Horse of Hanover on a scroll inscribed 'The King's'. The 6th 'rifle' battalion wore a bugle horn surmounted by a Lancashire Rose; the 8th 'Irish' battalion a crowned harp on a wreath of shamrocks, with the number and title. The Liverpool Scottish had the horse imposed on a cross of St. Andrew, with thistle sprays, and the words 'Liverpool Scottish' on a scroll. The Liverpool Pals (17th, 18th,19th and 20th battalions) wore the crest of the Earl of Derby with the motto 'Sans Changer' on a scroll at the base.
The Queen's	The Paschal Lamb bearing a swallow tailed flag, above a scroll inscribed 'The Queen's'.		
The Buffs	A dragon above a scroll inscribed 'The Buffs'.		
King's Own (Lancaster)	The Lion of England on a bar inscribed 'The King's Own'.		
Northumberland Fusiliers	Flaming grenade on which is St. George slaying the dragon, and a circlet bearing the inscription 'Northumberland Fusiliers'. The Tyneside Scottish (20th, 21st, 22nd, 23rd and 29th) battalions wore a cross of St Andrew within a thistle wreath, on which was a tower, lion and the inscription 'Tyneside Scottish'.	The Norfolks	A seated figure of Britannia in a laurel wreath, above a scroll inscribed 'The Norfolk Regiment'.
		The Lincolnshires	A sphinx resting on a tablet inscribed 'Egypt' in gothic lettering, under which is a scroll inscribed 'Lincolnshire'. The 4th and 5th battalions omitted the word 'Egypt'.
Warwickshires	Chained antelope standing above a scroll inscribed 'Royal Warwickshire'. The		

The Devonshires	An eight pointed star the topmost point of which is covered by a crown. In the centre Exeter castle surrounded by a circlet inscribed 'The Devonshire Regiment'.
The Suffolks	The Castle and Key of Gibraltar within a circlet on which is inscribed 'Montis Insignia Calpe', surmounted by a crown and within an oak wreath. Underneath a scroll inscribed 'The Suffolk Regt.'
Somerset Light Inf.	A bugle, in the strings of which are the letters 'PA' surmounted by a mural crown, above all of which is a scroll inscribed 'Jellalabad'.
West Yorkshires	Horse of Hanover with scroll beneath, inscribed 'West Yorkshire'. The Leeds Pals (15th battalion) wore the arms of the city of Leeds instead.
East Yorkshires	An eight pointed star, in the centre a rose surrounded by a laurel wreath. Underneath a scroll inscribed 'East Yorkshire'.
Bedfordshires	A Maltese cross on an eight pointed star, upon which is a garter, with a hart crossing a ford at the centre. At the bottom a scroll inscribed 'Bedfordshire'.
Leicestershires	A tiger over which appears the word 'Hindustan' and under which is a scroll inscribed 'Leicestershire'. 'Hindustan' omitted for 4th, 5th and 6th battalions.
Royal Irish	Harp surmounted by a crown, under which is a scroll inscribed 'The Royal Irish Regiment'.
Yorkshire Regiment	Cross (Dannebrog) and letter 'A' surmounted by a crown, under which is a tablet with the word 'Yorkshire'. At the base a scroll

	inscribed 'The Princess of Wales's Own Regt' and a rose. The 7th and 8th battalions took a cross surmounted by a crown with the words 'Leeds Rifles'. The former with, the latter without, a laurel wreath.
Lancashire Fusiliers	Flaming grenade on which is a sphinx within a laurel wreath; below the grenade a scroll inscribed 'Lancashire Fusiliers'. Most battalions have the word 'Egypt' on the tablet on which the sphinx rests, 4th, 5th and 6th battalions do not.
Royal Scots Fusiliers	Flaming grenade on which appears the Royal Arms.
Cheshire Regiment	Acorn and oak leaves on an eight pointed star. Scroll inscribed 'Cheshire'.
Royal Welsh Fusiliers	Flaming grenade, on the ball of which is a circlet inscribed 'Royal Welsh Fusiliers'; at the centre Prince of Wales plumes, coronet and motto. (Spelling Welch not introduced until 1920.)
South Wales Borderers	A wreath of the Immortelles, with the letters 'SWB' at the base. In the centre a sphinx resting on a tablet with the word 'Egypt'.
Scottish Borderers	A cross of St Andrew, with a circlet inscribed 'King's Own Scottish Borderers'. In the centre Edinburgh castle, and above and below the circlet two scrolls inscribed 'In veritate religionis confido', and 'Nisi Dominus frustra', all surrounded by a thistle wreath and topped by a crested crown.
Cameronians (rifles)	A 'mullet' or five pointed star, over a strung bugle, within a spray of thistles. The 5th bat-

	talion includes the number '5'.	Worcestershires	An eight pointed star upon which appears the garter and the Lion of England. Underneath the star is a tablet with the word 'Firm', under this a scroll inscribed 'Worcestershire'.
R. Inniskilling Fusiliers	Flaming grenade, bearing Inniskilling castle, and a scroll inscribed 'Inniskilling'.		
Gloucesters	A sphinx on a tablet inscribed 'Egypt', above two sprays of laurel. Beneath these a scroll inscribed 'Gloucestershire'. Worn with a small sphinx in a laurel wreath on the back of the headgear. The 5th and 6th battalions omit the word 'Egypt'.	East Lancashires	A sphinx on a tablet inscribed 'Egypt', above a rose, within a laurel wreath. Above the wreath is a crown, below the wreath a scroll inscribed 'East Lancashire'. The 4th and 5th battalions omit the word 'Egypt', but include a 'South Africa 1900-02' battle honour.
		East Surreys	An eight pointed star, the topmost point covered by a crown. At the centre the arms of Guildford on a shield, at the base a scroll inscribed 'East Surrey'. 6th battalion, Maltese cross and 'South Africa' battle honour variation; 15th (Wandsworth) battalion had the eight pointed star but

A selection of original cloth divisional insignia . Top left, 25th Division (New Army), red and white rectangles variant; top centre left, the Earl of Derby crest of 30th Division (New Army); top centre right, the acorn, diamond and cockerel of 40th Division (New Army); top right, the red rose of 55th (West Lancs) Division (Territorial Force). At the bottom is a staff arm band bearing the red horseshoe of 25th Division, which was also seen as a divisional sign worn on the back of Service Dress. Queen's Lancashire Regiment.

British and Indian Military Mounted Police, pictured in February 1917, wearing the red on black 'M.P.' arm band in the approved manner on the right upper arm. Authority is leant by the use of officer style Sam Browne belts, revolver holsters, whistles and chains. 14th/20th King's Hussars Collection

substituted the arms of Wandsworth, and had an extra scroll reading 'We Serve'.

D of Cornwall's L.I.   Bugle surmounted by a coronet, with scroll inscribed 'Cornwall'.

West Riding   Crest of the Duke of Wellington featuring a lion, coronet and motto, above a scroll inscribed 'The West Riding'.

Border Regt.   Eight pointed star, topmost point concealed by a crown, and on the star a cross surrounded by a laurel wreath, on each arm of which appear battle honours. In the centre of the cross is a dragon, the circlet around which reads 'Arroyo dos Molinos'. At the bottom of the star a scroll inscribed 'The Border Regt'. 4th and 5th battalion variations, crosses with 'South Africa' battle honours. 11th battalion wore the arms of the Earl of Lonsdale with a scroll inscribed '11th Battalion Border Regiment'.

Royal Sussex   The star of the Order of the Garter, topped with the Roussillon plume. At the base a scroll inscribed 'The Royal Sussex Regt.' 5th battalion variation with Maltese cross and arms of the cinque ports.

Hampshires   Royal tiger above a rose, all surrounded by a laurel wreath, with a scroll inscribed 'Hampshire'. 6th and 7th battalion variations, the former showing a ducal coronet and a strap inscribed 'Duke of Connaught's Own' within a laurel wreath, with a rose at the

	centre: the latter a dog gauge with a crown over, surrounded by a laurel wreath and battalion title. 8th battalion 'Isle of Wight Rifles' variation showing a castle.	Oxford and Bucks	Light Infantry bugle horn with strings. Buckinghamshire battalion variation with swan on Maltese cross.
South Staffordshires	Staffordshire knot surmounted by a crown, above a scroll inscribed 'South Staffordshire'.	Essex Regiment	Castle and Key of Gibraltar, surrounded by oak leaves. Beneath is a scroll inscribed 'The Essex Regt.', above a sphinx resting on a tablet bearing the word 'Egypt'. 4th, 5th, 6th and 7th battalions lack 'Egypt', but carry a 'South Africa' battle honour.
Dorsets	Sphinx on a tablet inscribed 'Marabout', over the Castle and Key of Gibraltar, below which a scroll inscribed 'Primus in Indis'. All surrounded by a laurel wreath with the word 'Dorsetshire' around the top. 4th battalion variation lacking 'Marabout'.		
		Notts and Derbyshire	Maltese cross surmounted by a crown; at the centre a stag in a wreath. Scrolls reading 'Sherwood Foresters' and at the base 'Derbyshire'. 7th 'Robin Hood' battalion includes that title, and a wreath around the cross, also a bugle rather than a stag.
South Lancashires	Prince of Wales's plumes, coronet and motto, over a sphinx resting on a tablet inscribed 'Egypt'. Above a scroll inscribed 'South Lancashire' and below another marked 'Prince of Wales's Vols.' Scrolls connected at either end with laurels. 4th battalion variation without 'Egypt'.		
		Loyals	Royal crest with crown above Lancashire Rose, all on a scroll reading 'Loyal North Lancashire'.
Welsh Regiment	Prince of Wales plumes, coronet and motto over a scroll inscribed 'The Welsh' (spelling 'Welch' not introduced until 1920). Cardiff Pals (16th battalion) wore the arms of Cardiff with scrolls reading 'Deffro mae'n Ddydd' and 'Y ddraig goch ddyry gychwyn'.	Northamptonshires	Castle and key of Gibraltar, above which is a scroll inscribed 'Gibraltar'; below a scroll with 'Talavera'. All in a wreath with 'Northamptonshire' at the base. 4th battalion, battalion title and 'South Africa' honour.
		Berkshires	Chinese dragon above a scroll inscribed 'Royal Berkshire'.
Black Watch	Star of the Order of the Thistle, on which appears a thistle wreath; within is an oval bearing the motto 'Nemo me impune lacesset' (or 'lacessit'). Above the oval appears a crown; within it is St Andrew and beneath it a sphinx. Two scrolls are inscribed respectively 'The Royal Highlanders', and, 'Black watch'. 4th, 5th, 6th and 7th battalion variations without sphinx.	West Kents	White horse of Kent over a scroll inscribed 'Invicta' in gothic lettering. Beneath this another scroll reading 'Royal West Kent'.
		Yorkshire Light Inf.	French horn around a Yorkshire Rose.
		Shropshire Light Inf.	Strung bugle horn with the letters 'K.S.L.I.' in the centre.

Middlesex Regiment	Prince of Wale's plumes, coronet and motto, above the coronet and cypher of the Duke of Cambridge, all within a laurel wreath. Two scrolls reading 'Albuhera' and 'Middlesex Regt.' 7th, 8th and 9th battalions with 'South Africa' variation. 18th battalion variation with scroll inscribed 'Public Works Pioneer Battalion'.
King's Royal Rifles	Maltese cross, on the centre of which is a bugle with a circlet around it inscribed 'The King's Royal Rifle Corps'. On the top arm of the cross a tablet inscribed 'Celer et Audax'.
Wiltshire Regiment	A cross patée bearing the cypher of the Duke of Edinburgh, topped with a ducal coronet. Under the cross a scroll inscribed 'The Wiltshire Regiment'.
Manchesters	The arms of the city of Manchester, below which is a scroll inscribed 'Manchester'.
North Staffordshires	Stafford knot with Prince of Wale's plumes, under which is a scroll inscribed 'North Stafford'.
York and Lancasters	Royal tiger with a rose above, with laurel sprays, a coronet at top, and below a scroll inscribed 'York and Lancaster'.
Durham Light Inf.	Strung bugle with crown above, within the string the letters 'DLI'.
Highland Light Inf.	Star of the Order of the Thistle, on which is a bugle horn and the letters 'HLI'. Crown at top, with an elephant and a scroll inscribed 'Assaye' at the bottom. 5th, 7th and 8th battalions, blank scroll or battle honour 'South Africa 1900-1902'. 9th 'Glasgow Highland' battalion has motto 'Nemo me impune

	lacessit', St. Andrew and cross, and battalion number, but no elephant or bugle.
Seaforth Highlanders	Stag's head above a scroll inscribed 'Cuidich'n Righ'. 5th battalion, a wild cat within a circlet or strap inscribed 'Sans peur': with feathers for officers.
Gordon Highlanders	The Marquis of Huntly's crest, with stag's head and ducal coronet within ivy wreath. Scroll at base inscribed 'By Dand'.
Cameron Highlanders	St Andrews cross within thistle wreath. Scroll at base inscribed 'Cameron'.
Royal Irish Rifles	Harp surmounted by a crown, underneath which is a scroll inscribed 'Quis Separabit'. 14th battalion 'Young Citizens' wore a shamrock and crown instead.
Royal Irish Fusiliers	Flaming grenade on which is a harp and Prince of Wales's feathers. Above a coronet.
Connaught Rangers	A harp surmounted by a crown, below which a scroll inscribed 'Connaught Rangers'.
Argyll and Sutherland	A circlet inscribed 'Argyll and Sutherland' within a wreath of thistles. In the centre the 'L' monogram of Princess Louise, with boar's head and cat to the left and right respectively. On the top of the circlet a coronet. The 8th battalion had a scroll with '8th A&SH'.
Leinster Regiment	Prince of Wales's plumes, coronet and motto; at the base a scroll inscribed 'The Leinster'.
Munster Fusiliers	Flaming grenade, on the ball of which is a tiger on a scroll inscribed 'Royal Munster'.

Two soldiers with a civilian friend, 1918. The man on the left wears the cap badge of the Royal Sussex Regiment and the black and white chequer board sign of 34th Division (New Army) on his right upper arm.

A soldier of a mounted unit wearing the white over blue 'Signal Service' arm band.

Dublin Fusiliers	As above, but tiger over elephant, and below the grenade a scroll inscribed 'Royal Dublin Fusiliers'.
Rifle Brigade	Cross within a laurel wreath surmounted by a crown. Battle honours on the arms of the cross, and two tablets above and below the cross inscribed 'Waterloo' and 'Peninsula' respectively. In the centre a circlet inscribed 'Rifle Brigade' and a bugle.
Honourable Arty. Comp.	Flaming grenade with 'HAC' on the ball.
Monmouthshires	Welsh dragon standing on ground. Some variations with

scroll and battalion title.

Herefordshires	Either the arms of the city of Hereford, or the lion from the crest of the city, with or without scroll inscribed 'Hereford'.
Hertfordshires	A hart within a circlet, crown above. Inscription 'The Hertfordshire Regiment'.
Cambridgeshires	A bridge with the arms of Ely superimposed, on a scroll inscribed 'The Cambridgeshire Regiment'.
London Regiment	1st-4th battalions, flaming grenade with garter, garter rose and crown on the ball. 5th battalion, Royal Arms in oak leaf wreath, with crown above, mace and sword, and scroll inscribed 'Primus in Urbe'. 6th battalion,

Maltese cross, 'South Africa' battle honour and battalion title. 7th 'City' battalion, flaming grenade with '7' on the ball. 8th 'Post Office Rifles', Maltese cross in wreath, 'South Africa' battle honour and battalion title. 9th, Maltese cross, 'South Africa' and battalion title 'Queen Victoria's'. 11th and 12th, Maltese crosses with appropriate titles. 13th, arms of Kensington on an eight pointed star. 14th 'London Scottish', thistle wreath with St. Andrew's cross, lion and circlet. Motto 'strike sure', and battalion title. 15th 'Civil service', Prince of Wales's plumes coronet and motto. 16th 'Westminsters', Maltese cross with portcullis at centre and title. 17th, Maltese cross in wreath, crown above, bugle in centre of circlet inscribed 'Rifle Brigade', 'South Africa' honour on arms of cross. 18th 'London Irish Rifles', crowned harp. 19th 'St Pancras', cross within wreath, crown above, numerals 'XIX' within centre circlet bearing battalion title. 20th Blackheath and Woolwich, White Horse of Kent with scrolls reading 'Invicta' and '20th Batt, The London Regt'. 21st, cross with crown, battalion titles, date '1803'. 22nd (and 24th), Paschal Lamb and scroll inscribed 'Queen's'. 23rd, eight pointed star with top covered by crown and arms of Guildford to centre, 'South Africa' honour and battalion title. 25th, number '25' on a wheel within a circlet inscribed 'County of London Cyclists', surrounded by laurel wreath with crown above and motto 'Tenax et audax'. 28th 'Artists Rifles' heads of Mars and Minerva, with scroll bearing battalion title underneath.

Corps and Artillery

Royal Artillery	Crowned field gun: mottos 'Ubique' and 'Quo fas et gloria ducunt', also variations.
Royal Engineers	The Garter with Royal cypher to centre, surrounded with a laurel wreath and a crown to top. Across base of the wreath scroll inscribed 'Royal Engineers'.
Royal Flying Corps	Letters 'RFC' within a laurel wreath surmounted by a crown.
Army Service Corps	Eight pointed star, top point covered by crown; Garter and monogram 'ASC' to centre, also minor variations.
R. A. Medical Corps	Rod of Aesculapius with serpent entwined, within a laurel wreath surmounted by a crown. Scroll at base inscribed 'Royal Army Medical Corps'.
Ordnance Corps	(Royal 1918) Shield with Ordnance Arms, that is, three cannons and three shot, over a scroll inscribed 'Army Ordnance Corps'.
Tank Corps	Tank in wreath, with crown over. Scrolls 'Tank' and 'Corps'.
Machine Gun Corps	Crossed machine guns, with crown over.
Pay Corps	Monogram 'APC' with crown over.
Veterinary Corps	Monogram 'AVC', within laurel wreath surmounted by a crown.
Remount Service	Horse surrounded by a strap, on which is inscribed 'Army Remount Service'. Crown to top.
School of Musketry	Crossed rifles surmounted by crown.

Military Police	Royal cypher within wreath topped by crown. Also with scroll 'Military Police'.
Women's A. Aux. Corps	Letters 'WAAC' in laurel wreath.
Chaplains	Christian: cross on square back ground surmounted by crown. Jewish: Star of David with and without crown.

British divisional signs, Western Front, 1918

As has been noted Divisional signs were widely introduced in 1916, but not all units employed divisional signs actually on uniform, and some changed their signs, neither were details such as backing colours entirely consistent. It is also true that a number of divisions used different signs on vehicles and HQs, and that although most signs were applied to the sleeve of the Service Dress some were sewn onto the back, or painted on the helmet. These were often also supplemented (or supplanted) on a uniform by a system of battle patches which distinguished brigade and battalion. The following list therefore contains only the most commonly used sign for each division, and notes by means of an asterisk (*) those known to have been worn on uniform or head gear by at least some of the troops.

Those readers wishing a more thorough explanation should consult V. Wheeler-Holohan *Divisional and Other Signs*, London, 1920, and M. Chappell *British Battle Insignia*, London, 1986.

1st Cavalry	White oblong with red vertical stripe.*
2nd Cavalry	Two horseshoes.
3rd Cavalry	Three horse shoes.
Guards Division	Open eye.
1st (Regular)	Red or white spot on small flag.
2nd (Regular)	Three eight pointed stars, white, red and white.
3rd (Regular)	Circle and cross in yellow.*
4th (Regular)	Ram's head.*
5th (Regular)	Blue square with yellow diagonal bar.
6th (Regular)	White circle.*
8th (Regular)	Red square within white square.*
9th Scottish (New Army)	Blue thistle, or thistle on blue.*
11th Northern (New Army)	Red circle over triangle 'keyhole' shape.*
12th Eastern (New Army)	Ace of spades.*
14th Light (New Army)	Two intersecting white lines on green.
15th Scottish (New Army)	Red wedge on white within black ring*.
16th Irish (New Army)	Shamrock.*
17th Northern (New Army)	White dot and dash on red.*
18th Eastern (New Army)	Letters 'ATN'.
19th Western (New Army)	Butterfly.*
20th Light (New Army)	Black cross, red dot to centre.
21st (New Army)	Three sevens radiating from a central point.
24th (New Army)	Four triangles in white, radiating from a white square on red.
25th (New Army)	Red horseshoe.*
29th (Regular)	Red triangle.*
30th (New Army)	White on black Earl of Derby crest.*
31st (New Army)	Red and white roses on black ground.*
32nd (New Army)	Five red circles.*
33rd (New Army)	Double three domino.*
34th (New Army)	Black and white chequer board.*
35th (New Army)	Circle of seven fives.
36th Ulster (New Army)	Red hand of Ulster.*
37th (New Army)	Yellow horseshoe.*
38th Welsh (New Army)	Red dragon.*
39th (New Army)	Blue and white striped square.
40th (New Army)	Acorn on a diamond on a cockerel.*
41st (New Army)	White diagonal stripe on ground.
42nd East Lancashire (Territorial)	White over red diamond.*
46th North Midland (Territorial)	Red over green oblong.
47th London (Territorial)	White eight pointed star.
49th West Riding (Territorial)	White rose.

50th Northumbrian (Territorial) Red unicorn head.*

51st Highland (Territorial) Letters 'HD'.*

52nd Lowland (Territorial) Letter L and small St Andrew's shield.

55th West Lancashire (Territorial) Red rose.*

56th London (Territorial) Vertical sword.*

57th West Lancashire (Territorial) White horizontal line through red arch.*

58th London (Territorial) A tower.*

59th North Midland (Territorial) Three yellow crosses superimposed.

61st South Midland (Territorial) Roman numerals 'LXI' superimposed.

62nd West Riding (Territorial) Pelican.

63rd Royal Naval An anchor (amongst other things).*

A staff officer demonstrates a German helmet and trench armour to his majesty King George V, Vimy Ridge, July 1917. In addition to a staff arm band and a patch at the top of the sleeve, the man with his back to the camera wears the red dragon of the 38th (Welsh) Division between his shoulder blades. On the ground are two officers' steel helmets with rank badges affixed to the front and neatly tailored khaki covers.
IWM Q 5673

66th East Lancashire (Territorial) Blue triangle with yellow central bar.

74th (Yeomanry) Broken spur on red diamond.*

Special Clothing and Equipment

From the first winter of the war onwards came a plethora of new articles of clothing, both official and unofficial. Balaclavas, jerseys, mittens and waterproof sheets were already on issue, but the myriads of 'unofficial' knitted socks, mufflers, cardigans and waistcoats made personally by well wishers, or purchased from civilian outfitters, are unlikely to ever be satisfactorily quantified. Sometimes charitable or patriotic organisations sent out numerous parcels of clothing. Private A.S. Dolden of the London Scottish recorded how he received a package from the Queen Alexandra Field Force Fund which contained, amongst other sundries, a towel, mittens, muffler, 'sleeping helmet', handkerchief and spare boot laces. One officer described, even when sleeping in the trenches in summer, how he wore Service Dress, an other ranks greatcoat, 'Jaeger' cardigan, and his mother's old scarf. When it got really cold the same man later went on to ask for and receive from home a 'sort of enormous seaman's jersey', thigh length, and 'almost up to the ears'. Satisfactory though this was, he then purchased a leather waistcoat, long leather 'trench boots', and a 'simply ripping' British warm coat. Exactly how much of this could be crammed on at any one time was not recorded.

The humble sand bag rapidly assumed a hundred and one uses, sartorial and otherwise. A number of memoirs record how they were tied around the lower leg in muddy conditions, providing an extra layer whilst being easy to take off in comparison to the effort of an uncomfortable half hour spent removing and cleaning a pair of puttees. Sand bags were also used to carry bombs and kit, and less successfully employed for shifting rations. Some soldiers improvised pillows from them; others folded one inside the helmet as a cushion; a few wore them on their heads.

Fur waistcoats of various descriptions, often actually of goat skin, were officially and widely adopted in the first winter of the war. Although these were worn both fur inward, and fur outward, the 'proper' way of wearing them was always hair side outside, as was noted in a General Routine Order of January 1915, which stated that the skin itself was likely to become 'brittle and hard' if exposed directly to the weather, whereas the fur helped to 'throw off water'. Photographic evidence shows that sometimes fur jackets with sleeves were also worn. An unpredicted hazard of these natural furs was their appalling smell.

In 1915 many units also got a special official issue of heavy duty gloves. Each infantry battalion was entitled to receive 48 pairs, with greater numbers going to the Royal Engineers and lesser numbers to the Royal Artillery. Presumably these 'Gloves, Hedging' were not only intended for dealing with trees and foliage, but were also useful for dealing with tricky stores such as barbed wire. At about the same time extra issues of warm clothing made Field Ambulances and Clearing Hospitals just a shade more homely: these garments included 'Pyjama Suits', bed socks and 'Warm bedroom slippers'.

The 'Winter Scale' of clothing which pertained from 15 October 1916 officially sanctioned the following articles of clothing over and above the ordinary Service Dress for the infantryman: a 'waterproof cover' for the peaked cap or Tam O'Shanter; a 'cap comforter' or soft woollen knitted cap; 'Coat, great, dismounted'; two pairs of woollen 'drawers'; woollen vest; worsted gloves; and the 'Waist coat, cardigan'. Highlanders became eligible for two pairs of 'drawers, short' but apparently only when 'recommended by the Medical Authorities'. Mounted troops were entitled to cord pantaloons and a mounted pattern greatcoat, but for some obscure reason were limited to a single pair of woollen drawers. Cyclists were listed as being issued 'Knickerbockers, cyclists' instead of Service Dress trousers, and a 'British Warm' and a cape instead of a great coat.

An additional 'Special Scale' made available extra

items of clothing to soldiers on specific duties. Fingerless gloves went to all infantry at the front; 'Coats sheepskin lined' or oilskins could be worn by certain categories of driver in lieu of the normal coat; leather jerkins or an 'undercoat fur' could be claimed by any troops at the front who did not have access to a sheepskin. Gum boots, as stocks allowed, were also given out as a 'trench store' to those actually in the trenches, but since they could easily be sucked off in mud they were not intended for use in the attack.

Some troops received special issues of clothing whatever the season. Royal Engineer 'Tunnelling Companies' for example were listed as being issued with 'Donkeys' in addition to service and fatigue dress, with 50 suits of oilskins per company, and either 'Gum Boots thigh' or 'short'. Machine Gun Companies and Lewis Gun Detachments were noted in early 1916 as being entitled to two special short reinforced 'Capes' per gun for carriage of the weapons. They were also, like trench mortar crews, allotted special gloves for handling their weapons when hot. Machine gunners; masks were also available, but never seem to have proved as popular or useful to the infantry and cavalry as they were later to the tanks.

Certain Army Service Corps personnel, including not only drivers and mechanics but meat handlers,

Army Ordnance Corps personnel demonstrate an interesting variety of special clothing at the Royal Army Clothing Department, June 1918. From left to right are: the 'Coat Sheepskin lined'; a fire resistant suit; a white 'boiler suit' style set of snow camouflage, complete with hood and helmet cover; flying helmets, short overcoat and life jacket. IWM Q 30788.

were entitled to 'Dungaree clothing'. Military Police were kitted out with a special waterproof cape, presumably because their duties involved endless standing around in all weathers. Dispatch riders, who had always been equipped with 'pantaloons' and two piece oversuits of jackets and leggings, also became entitled to extra clothes under the 'winter scales'. These additional garments were hand 'shields', issue sweaters, and a 'Coat Warm M.S.' (mounted services).

Some of the most interesting pieces of specialist clothing devised during the course of the war were those made with concealment and sniping in mind. One of the simplest was the head 'veil', a bag-like hood, with eye holes. Doubtless some were locally extemporised from cloth, but a simple alternative was a sandbag pulled over the head with the fibres separated to create vision slots. Two different Sealed Pattern veils, in respectively light and dark brown

In one of the best known photographs of the Great War a working party burdened with shovels stands in the mud near St. Pierre Divion, November 1916. Thigh length gum boots and ground sheets tied around the neck are worn as protection from the rain. IWM Q 4602.

material, were introduced in 1916. In 1917 *Notes For Infantry Officers* referred to the use of a rather different form of 'veil', in either green or brown gauze, dependent on the local background. Sniper officer Major F.M. Crum of the King's Royal Rifle Corps also mentioned the use of masks, sometimes of gauze and painted to represent brick.

According to the history of the Royal Engineers, sniper 'robes' or 'sniping suits' consisting of loose hooded blouses which reached to the knee and were painted to harmonise with their surroundings were first inspired by the French. These garments, which were sometimes also referred to as 'coats', were frequently teamed with camouflaged canvas rifle covers and gloves. Though some 'blouses' were doubtless made by other units, many were fabricated by the Engineers' own Camouflage Service in France, which employed artists, scenic artists, carpenters and 'cardboard workers' in its workshops, and grew into a significant enterprise during the course of 1916. The

appearance of each hand painted suit was obviously slightly different, but some clues as to appearance may be had by reference to the pallet of colours available in the R.E. stores. Though a range of no less than 20 hues was used at one time or another, those shades in most abundant supply were light 'Brunswick Green'; dark 'Brunswick Green'; yellow ochre; white, and 'Burnt Turkey Brown Umber'. Fortunately an excellent example of a sniper's robe survives in the Imperial War Museum collection: it is made of canvas with a separate hood, grass green in colour, and splattered with black, tan brown and white paint to create a disruptive pattern.

Though the long smock-like garment was a major step forward and of significant concealment value, its length made crawling a very tricky operation. Thought was therefore soon applied to other designs with shorter bodies, or one piece suits with legs, and a Sealed Pattern for a crawling suit was produced in 1916. By March 1918 the manual *Principles and Practice of Camouflage*, noted two forms of camouflaged overall which were part of the stocks being administered by the Corps Camouflage Officer within each Corps sector. These were a 'boiler suit' type, with a detachable scrim hood, rifle cover and gloves, and a very modern looking 'Symien' pattern sniper suit consisting entirely of loose fitting scrim, and comprising a jacket with hood attached, separate legs, rifle cover and gloves.

At least one source also mentions the use of the 'domino', a speckled hooded cape whose camouflage pattern rendered it particularly useful amongst trees. Snow suits, apparently usually of a boiler suit design with hood, were certainly also produced in both Britain and in France: photographs show them being used with a matching white helmet cover. 'Overalls for Night Patrols' of an unspecified pattern were on issue at a scale of ten sets per battalion of infantry at the front by the end of 1916, and the history of the 1/4th Battalion of the Loyal North Lancashires records that the attire for night raids soon became a 'boiler suit' and 'cap comforter' with all identifying material left safely behind. A sealed Pattern brown 'Night' overall appeared in 1917. By daylight all these types of camouflage clothing could be improved further to match the local surroundings with the use of straw, foliage and vegetable stalks as appropriate.

By the last year of war it was recognised that the work of Corps camouflage dumps was vital, and that the issue of concealment requisites should in no way be hindered by 'red tape'. To this ends it was decreed that 'no indents are required for any stock article. If it is actually available at the dump it will be issued

forthwith, if transport is sent to collect it.' The Royal Engineers alone recorded that they had supervised the manufacture of at least 4,795 sniper suits; 2,741 'dummy heads' to mislead German snipers; and 12, 553 dummy 'Chinese Attack' figures during the course of the war. This was in addition to almost one million square yards of painted canvas, over four million square yards of scrim, six million square yards of wire netting and seven million square yards of 'fish netting' which went into other camouflage projects.

Helmets and Body Armour

The disproportionate number of often lethal head wounds, and the appearance of the French 'Adrian' steel helmet in mid 1915, soon influenced the British to begin the process of designing and procuring their own protective headgear. The first moves of the 'Inventions Committee' established to look at the question were to order samples of steel skull caps, and to obtain a small quantity of French helmets for trials. These were received in late July 1915, and not long

A labour battalion working party pause for dinner on the Ancre sector, October 1916. In evidence are not only a wide variety of fur waistcoats but sacking helmet covers, mess tins, and rifle and pick collar badges. IWM Q 1600.

Sniper Team, Western Front, 1917.

By the middle of the war the snipers' trade had become highly organised as a branch of scouting and intelligence work with perhaps a dozen specially trained men per battalion maintaining a screen of observation and fire across the battalion front. Two man teams were usual with the better rifleman acting as the shooter, and the other man acting as observer, the pair would change roles when concentration lapsed. Off to the side above this post can be seen a metal loophole, likely to be one of several dummy positions in the vicinity. The firing will actually be done through one or more holes in the parapet camouflaged externally by tin cans and other detritus, and often screened off internally by curtains to prevent light showing. Where a post was maintained over a period it would be usual to keep written notes of the enemy positions, ranges and movements and pass these on to the snipers of the next battalion to occupy the sector.

In this painting the observer is watching through a No 9. Mark II box periscope, the top of which has been concealed by a sand bag. When not in use the periscope can be folded in half and put in the leather carrying case seen near the observer's knee. The observer wears Service Dress, steel helmet, parts of the 1914 Pattern equipment and leather jerkin. On his right upper arm appears the fleur-de-lis badge of the scout or sniper. Other impedimenta scattered around include shovels for digging out new tunnels through the parapet at night, a Royal Engineers made 'knobkerrie' and a box of grenades. This particular box has the old style rope handle on the top: others had a small handle at either end.

The sniper, left, is wearing a robe and hood closely based on a surviving example in the Imperial War Museum collection. The SMLE with offset telescopic sight is camouflaged with strips of cloth, and gloves to match the robe were sometimes worn. The robes and other equipment were specially painted with disruptive patches and splatters to match the surroundings in each local area. Boiler suit sniper clothing began to replace the coat or robe during the latter part of the war, but both were still in use in 1918. Painting by Christa Hook.

after it was recommended that a few French helmets be purchased specifically for the use of sentries in front line trenches. Though some officers did succeed in obtaining French helmets, the general adoption of the Adrian by British troops was overtaken by events at home because the War Office in London had by now come to the same conclusion as the army committee, and the forces in the field, and expedited its own experiments. The favoured solution was not to copy or buy the French helmet, which was considered both too weak and too complex, but to go for a distinctively British out and out 'Shrapnel helmet' designed first and foremost for the best protection from shrapnel shells bursting overhead and defence against falling objects.

The precise model of headgear selected was patented by the inventor John L. Brodie in August 1915. It consisted of the now familiar shallow steel bowl with liner and chin strap, soon to be christened by the troops variously as the 'battle bowler', 'trench hat', or plain old 'tin hat'. The key advantages of this piece of equipment were perceived to be its good coverage from above, and its ease of production, since the main shell of the hat could be stamped out from one piece of metal. The first model of 'Brodie' helmet to see service was the so called 'Type A', made of mild steel and with a brim which varied between 1.5 and 2 inches in width, depending on where such a measurement was taken, and a dome which was very slightly flattened on top. Production of this first model had not been under way more than a few weeks, when,

in October 1915, it was decided to upgrade the specification so that henceforth the helmet shell would be made of hardened manganese steel of the 'Hadfield' variety. This was to be capable of stopping a shrapnel ball travelling at a velocity of 750 feet per second. Though very tough this was still not robust enough to stop a close or medium range direct hit from rifle or machine gun, nor was it intended to be. This second or 'B' type helmet was distinguishable not only by the metallurgy, but by the relative narrowness of the brim, and the lack of flattening at the dome. Production of the old and new type helmets continued in parallel for some time whilst problems in fabricating with the new metal were worked out.

The first helmets began to arrive at the front in small quantities in September 1915. The scale of issue was initially set at just 50 per Battalion, and the earliest examples were not issued to one particular man but kept centrally by units to be used as 'Trench Stores'. The unit would utilise them whilst actually in the line, and they would be retained there to be used by the next battalion in the sector. On 9 December 1915 a question regarding steel helmets was asked in the House of Commons to which the Under Secretary of State for War replied that he knew 'no reason why the troops should not be wearing the steel helmets issued to them'. It was a classic piece of double speak, since in fact most troops had not been issued with anything by that time. There was also an ugly rumour circulating that some generals were reluctant to hand out what helmets there were as they looked stupid and

Officers and men of 1/8th (Irish) Battalion The King's (Liverpool Regiment) pictured the night after a trench raid near Wailly, April 1916. The remarkable variety of headgear includes not only captured German Pickelhauben but many different forms of balaclava and 'cap comforter', and Service Dress caps worn back to front. Also in evidence are scarves, a dark jersey, gloves, and the use of face blacking. The Irish harp collar badges of two of the officers can be seen. IWM Q 510.

Left.

Privates Savery and Battersby of the South Lancashire Regiment wearing winter goat skins and balaclavas at La Clytte, 1915. Queen's Lancashire Regiment.

would make the men 'soft'. One wag observed that the Brodie was obviously designed by a man with a 'massively developed brain' and Zeppelin attack in mind. For Edmund Blunden the 'dethronement' of the soft cap and the appearance of the 'curious green mushroom' of the steel helmet symbolised the change that was coming over the war; from 'personal crusade' to 'vast machine of violence'. Yet whatever its drawbacks, the steel helmet led immediately to a reduction in head injuries.

Colour schemes for these early helmets appear to

An interesting study of an Army Service Corps driver, c.1916, sporting not only the Coat Sheepskin Lined, but the 1914 padded winter variant of the Service Dress cap with its distinctive flap.

have varied somewhat. Brodie himself recommended a softly melded mixture of mottled light green, blue and orange, which, after application gave a vaguely verdigrised bronze effect of varying shades of green and khaki. More common was a rather shiny blue-grey, or green, which the troops sometimes contrived to render less conspicuous with either a sand bag cover or mud. By early 1916, about a quarter of a million helmets had been made, but though perceived as a great success, the original Brodie was not without its faults. General Plumer, for example, commented that the headgear was too shallow, the lining too slippery, the surface too reflective, and the edge of the rim too sharp. From May 1916 began the issue of a new type of helmet, subsequently designated the 'Mark I' which incorporated a two part liner and a thin mild steel folded rim which made the edge of the brim less sharp. Just as importantly the helmet exterior was now painted khaki, the texture being roughened by an application of saw dust or sand whilst still wet. The result was an excellent matt and non-reflective surface.

The use of a sacking hood camouflaged with foliage.

Though there would be other minor changes to the lining, the 'Mark I' would see out the war. Eventually every soldier received his own steel helmet, and production was such that many were supplied to America, and they were also issued in limited quantities on the Home Front.

Interestingly there were still many minor variations to be seen. Perhaps most significantly, though the Mark I was less conspicuous than its predecessors, helmet covers continued to be quite widely worn.

These were made in France and by manufacturers at home, the British produced examples being generally of better quality, and consisting of four panels of khaki drill material tightened over the helmet by means of a drawstring. Officers often took advantage of private purchases, and elegantly bedecked helmets with the marks of London tailors and outfitters inside are by no means unusual. Helmets were also painted or stencilled with badges of rank, divisional signs, and copies of regimental cap badges and symbols. Amongst the many regimental and corps devices seen in contemporary photographs are the Royal Army Medical Corps rod of Aesculapius with its entwined serpent within a wreath, topped by a crown; the famous yellow hackle of the Lancashire Fusiliers; the bugle horns of the King's Shropshire Light Infantry and King's Own Yorkshire Light Infantry; the Elephant of the Duke of Wellington's Regiment; the Grenadier Guards 'flaming grenade'; and the gun symbol of the Royal Artillery.

Some units even went so far as to drill holes in the fronts of their helmets and attach metal cap badges. This practice soon met with rebuke and a ban in the *Routine Orders* for it weakened the structural integrity of the helmet. Nevertheless certain examples of this method of identification do survive both in photographs and amongst museum artifacts. One particularly interesting piece, worn by Lieutenant J.E. Blumenfield of the 3rd King's Own Hussars at Cambrai, is on display in the regimental museum at the Lord Leycester Hospital, Warwick. In this case the running horse badge of the regiment is worn on the front of the helmet on a light blue painted rectangle.

Rather more rarely seen on the helmet was an eye defence devised by Captain Cruise of the RAMC, occulist to the King. This consisted of a metal rod fitted under the brim of the helmet and a chain mail visor made of closely woven links which was drawn taught. According to one report this did not get a good reception at the front and was said to produce a sensation of dizziness as the movement of the helmet caused the position of the links of the visor to alter in relation to the eyes as the wearer walked around. Even so the Cruise visor was used to a limited extent in 1916 and 1917.

Although body armour never achieved the universality of the steel helmet it was seen with reasonable frequency in the trenches, both as a private purchase item, and as a small scale experimental and

Line drawing of the 'Boiler' sniper suit, with scrim hood, as depicted in the camouflage manual of 1918.

Contemporary line drawing of the 'Symien' scrim sniper suit.

The Boiler Sniper Suit,
With painted transparent scrim hood

The Symien Sniper Suit,
Painted transparent scrim throughout.

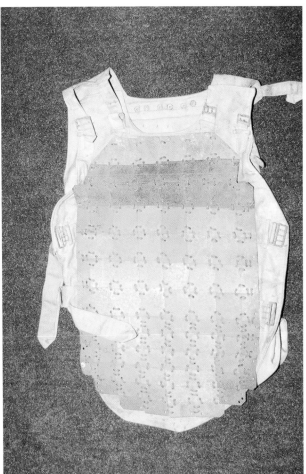

The Mark I steel helmet, pictured together with a Glengarry of the Cameronians which was manufactured by J. Angus and Company, 1915. The helmet has been painted with the signs of 25th Division (New Army) which included units from a wide geographical area. In 1917 this formation had three battalions of the Cheshires; two each of the Loyal North Lancashires and South Lancashires; and one from the Wiltshires; Royal Irish Rifles; Border Regiment; and Lancashire Fusiliers. Their pioneer battalion was drawn from the South Wales Borderers. M.S. & G.C.

The rather ineffective Franco-British body armour, made of scales secured to a khaki backing. German officer Ernst Jünger recorded how a bullet could easily drive the small plates into the hapless wearer's body. Queen's Lancashire Regiment.

official issue. One of the earliest types to come to formal notice was the so called 'Franco-British' body armour, a coat of plates which was apparently also worn with 'splinter goggles' and a cylindrical steel hat. By March 1915 the possibility of an official issue 'shield' for scouts and bombers was under consideration, mainly as a result of suggestions from private inventors, although the High Command seems pretty rapidly to have formed the conclusion that anything actually 'bullet proof' was going to be so heavy that it would be impractical. It was therefore thought that experiment should concentrate on finding a suitable garment for stopping lower velocity missiles like grenade splinters and shrapnel balls. This direction was duly adopted by the Trench Warfare

Section of the Munition Design Committee, which also produced various models of 'trench loops' or 'snipers plates' which were to be used as static cover.

In the autumn and winter of 1915 more than 40 different substances were put to the test with materials as diverse as silk, manganese steel, rubber, 'woodite', felt and resinated linen all coming under scrutiny as to their suitability and ballistic performance. The result of all this activity was that experimental issues of 'Dayfield' steel splinter proof armour in khaki fabric covers were made in June 1916, and that a request was made for an issue of 400 sets per Division two months later. These began to appear at the front in regular weekly instalments until June 1917 when a lighter pattern was substituted. In 1918 there were also experiments with smaller areas of protection for vital organs, such as a plate in the respirator bag, and an armoured entrenching tool head. One result of these and other efforts would be the so called 'E.O.B.' corselet which bore a resemblance to later bomb

Men of the West Yorkshires pose in their new 'Brodie' steel helmets, 1916. Notice also the detail of the boots and Pattern 1914 leather equipment.

disposal suits.

In parallel with these official activities private manufacturers and worried relatives also did their best to encourage the 'private purchase' market. Photographs, advertising materials and surviving examples all suggest that there was a small but steady influx of many different models of unofficial defences to the trenches. Amongst these was the 'Chemico' body shield which was a side fastening waistcoat with two pockets at waist level and a crotch defence attached: unlike most of the others the 'Chemico' was not made of metal, but was an inch thick sandwich of many layers of different materials including linen, cotton and silk. The 'Flexible Armour Guard' was a product of John Berkley of Newcastle and had a light breast and back of small square plates riveted to a canvas support. It was easy to wear but effective only against the slowest moving of fragments, whilst bullets had the alarming tendency to push the little plates into the hapless wearer's body. 'Wilkinson's Safety Service Jacket' was only slightly more effective, but was very light at just 3lb and as a small waistcoat was quite

unobtrusive beneath the Service Dress Jacket. Another defence which aimed at ease of movement was the 7 lb 'Featherweight'; again it was only partially efficacious but it did cover much of the body as it was slipped over the shoulders like a tabard, and also included a 'sporran plate' for the groin.

A number of commercial designs also took on board the fact that it was very difficult to cover the whole body effectively without becoming prohibitively weighty. Some defences therefore just covered a smaller vital area by means of a single, or at most a few, thicker plates. These armours included the 'Portobank' which in fact was a sandwich construction of steel, felt and wadding; the 'Corelli' which was said to be able to stop pretty well anything including rifle bullets at six paces but weighed 17.5 lb, and the remarkable 'Roneo-Miris' body shield. This metal oval was secured by straps over the shoulders, round the waist, and under the crotch, as well it might be since it weighed a staggering 22 lb.

Equipment

The standard personal equipment of the infantry was the Pattern 1908 web equipment. This had been designed by Major Burrowes of the Royal Irish

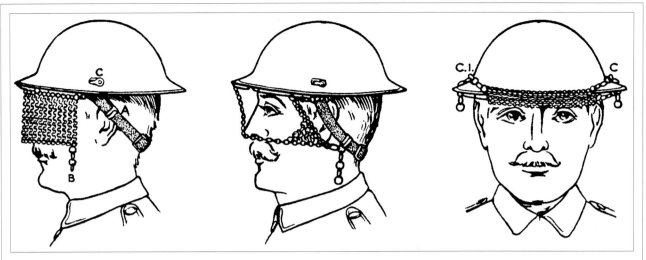

Diagrammatic representations of the chain mail 'Cruise' visor and the ways in which it could be worn.

Fusiliers in collaboration with the Mills Web Equipment company, and was presented to the Army's Equipment Sub Committee in 1906. Extensive trials led to acceptance in 1907, and a drive to re-equip the army accordingly. A full description of the new

An advertisement for the folding Pullman A.1. body shield, said to be proof against revolvers and shrapnel balls. Many of the armours in use were private purchases; this particular promotion appeared in the Buffs regimental magazine.

webbing appeared in the 1913 War Office official publication, *The Pattern 1908 Web Infantry Equipment*. According to this document the advantages of the 1908 Pattern equipment were: all parts of it were connected together allowing the whole to be taken off in one motion; it was well balanced; no constricting straps crossed the chest; and it was flexible enough to allow the load to be disposed of in a variety of ways. The equipment was throughout made of a specially waterproofed woven webbing, linked by tongueless

The 'featherweight' body shield, light at 7 lb, but less than proof even against pistol bullets.

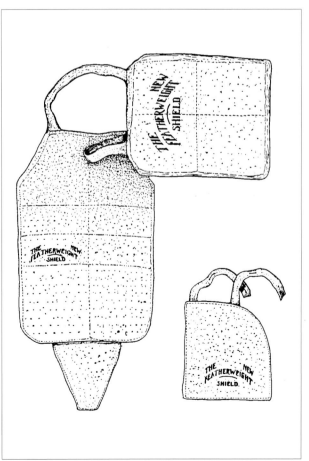

The Mark I steel helmet.

self locking buckles and consisting of more than a dozen different components.

The 'waist belt' was three inches wide and came in three different lengths, small, medium and large. The bayonet 'frog' was designed to accommodate the scabbard of the Pattern 1907 sword bayonet, and slipped onto the waist belt by means of a loop. The 'braces' were interchangeable, consisted of webbing straps 50 inches long and two inches wide, and carried sliding buckles for the attachment of the pack. The 'cartridge carriers' were not interchangeable, having a left and right, and each consisted of an assemblage of five 15-round pockets in two tiers, the flaps of which were secured by snap fasteners. The interior of each pocket was so divided that each would snugly accommodate three five-round chargers. Between them the pouches could accommodate a total of 150 rounds. A tendency for the lower left pouches to snag on trench parapets and drop their load was speedily identified, and in October 1914 a solution was announced in the *List of Changes* which cured the problem by the provision of sliding straps, instead of snaps, on these receptacles. Even so equipment sets with both the new and old type fasteners on the lower

left pouches continued to be used for a long time afterwards.

The main pack was approximately 15 inches long by 13 inches wide and secured shut by a folding flap with buckles; to the pack were attached two supporting straps 32 inches in length. The haversack was somewhat smaller at 11 inches by 9, and normally hung at the left hip, although it could be moved up to the back when the main pack was not worn. The water bottle carrier consisted of a skeleton framework of webbing secured by a snapped retaining strap. The helve carrier accommodated the handle for the entrenching tool which was usually fitted against the bayonet scabbard, and the head of the tool itself was contained in a bag carrier which hung on the belt over the right hip. According to Henry Ogle, then an other rank in the Warwickshires, the entrenching tool was an extremely versatile piece of kit: 'In action it was used as both a pick and a shovel, or its handle could form a little "Spanish Windlass" to tauten slack pairs of wires. When not in use the blade provided comforting defensive armour over one's otherwise vulnerable rear. Its more personal and domestic uses were many and various. It dug and afterwards covered up one's private latrine, scraped clean and smooth the ground in dugout and barn, chopped sticks and

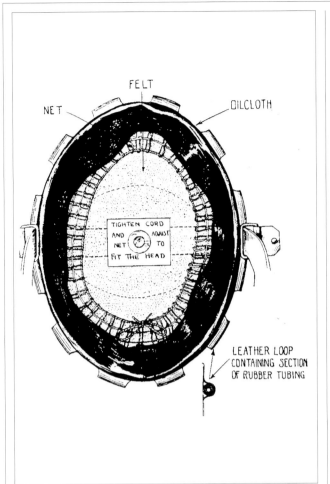

NET   FELT   OILCLOTH

TIGHTEN CORD
AND   ADJUST
NET   TO
FIT THE HEAD

LEATHER LOOP
CONTAINING SECTION
OF RUBBER TUBING

Above.

The lining of the Mark I steel helmet, and a sketch showing the various parts.

Right.

Detail showing the rolled over edge of the Mark I helmet and the rivet retaining the chin strap fitting.

hammered nails. Its well sharpened pick jabbed holes in a fire bucket, and if the glowing bucket had to be moved, was used as a carrying hook.'

That the 1908 Pattern equipment did its job was beyond question, and the arrangement of the whole as a jacket of straps and the balance afforded by the braces was a definite improvement on the 19th century systems which preceded it. A number of modifications were made during the life of this equipment, as for example the minor alterations to the haversack and bayonet frog fittings announced in 1909, but the only two significant changes were the alteration to the ammunition carrier closures already mentioned and the addition of a pistol holster to the ensemble. It is interesting to note that variations on the normal 1908 Pattern configuration of pouches are sometimes found: many of these are Canadian, Australian and other colonial types, but at least some with differing

A 6th Suffolk Sergeant's "Remarkable" Feat

Above.
An unusual view of a very important part of the infantryman's kit. In this case the munition boots of a sergeant of 6th Battalion the Suffolk Regiment. S.B.

Left.
The Pattern 1914 leather equipment, with its characteristic 'S' clasp belt and pair of 60 round leather ammunition pouches pictured, c. 1915. Note that this soldier is wearing a button in his hat in lieu of a proper cap badge.

numbers or types of ammunition carrier are British, and were most likely made up to satisfy demand from the many new battalions raised early in the war. Perhaps its greatest tribute was the fact that when troops were given the choice they would usually opt for the Pattern 1908 over the alternatives.

One would perhaps hesitate before calling the webbing 'popular', because some officers and NCOs differed from the sensible opinion of the manual compilers that the soldiery should be allowed to march with their jacket buttons open whenever they wished when carrying the webbing. Moreover the 'full marching order' load carried by the soldier at the start of the war, counting arms, ammunition, clothes, pack and equipment, was 61 lb. According to the *Field*

Sᴇʀɢᵗ. C Eᴠᴀɴs' Sǫᴜᴀᴅ, Gʀᴇɴᴀᴅɪᴇʀ Gᴜᴀʀᴅs, Dᴇᴄ 1916

Men of the Grenadier Guards wearing the Pattern 1908 equipment, December 1916. Note also the turned down cap visors, characteristic of the Guards regiments.

Service Pocket Book of 1914 this was made up as follows:

Clothing and other items worn by the soldier –

Boots, ankle, pair	4 lb	
Braces	0 lb	4½ oz
Cap, Service Dress (or Glengarry)	0 lb	9 oz
Disc, identity, with cord	0 lb	¼ oz
Drawers woollen, pair	1 lb	½ oz
Jacket, Service Dress, and metal titles, with field dressing	2 lb	8 oz
Knife clasp, with marlin spike and tin opener	0 lb	8 oz
Pay book (in right breast pocket of S.D. jacket)	0 lb	2 oz
Puttees, pair	0 lb	13 oz
Shirt	1 lb	2 oz
Socks, pair	0 lb	4½ oz
Trousers, Service Dress	2 lb	½ oz
Waistcoat, cardigan	1 lb	7 oz

Arms–
Rifle, with oil bottle, pull through,

and sling	8 lb	15¾ oz
Bayonet, and scabbard	1 lb	8¾ oz

Ammunition–
Cartridges, S.A. Ball .303 in,

150 rounds	9 lb	

Tools–
Implement, intrenching, Pattern 1908,

and carriers	2 lb	9¼ oz

Accoutrements–
Water bottle, Pattern 1908 web equipment,

with knife fork and spoon in haversack	8 lb	4¼ oz

Articles carried in the pack–

Cap, comforter	0 lb	4 oz
Holdall, containing laces, tooth brush, razor and case, shaving brush and comb	0 lb	9¼ oz
Greatcoat with metal titles	6 lb	10½ oz
Housewife [i.e. sewing kit]	0 lb	3¼ oz
Mess tin and cover	1 lb	6½ oz
Socks, worsted	0 lb	4½ oz
Soap	0 lb	3 oz
Towel, hand	0 lb	9 oz

Reconstruction showing the rear view of a typical battle order using elements of the 1908 Pattern webbing as it might have appeared in 1918. Here the haversack is worn on the back, teamed with a set of four Lewis gun ammunition pouches, two of which come to rest either side of the haversack. Notice the mess tin in its cover in the small of the back, and the enamel mug. Hanging below the waist are the bayonet, wire cutters and entrenching tool head in its cover. G.C.

"FULL MARCHING ORDER" WHAT YOUR KIT FEELS LIKE AFTER TEN MILES!

The cartoonist's view of the soldiers' burden. Many were weighed down mercilessly, but it should be remembered that the equipments in use in the Great War were better than those they replaced.

Rations and water–
Bread   0 lb   12 oz
Cheese   0 lb   3 oz
Iron ration, biscuit, preserved meat, tea,
sugar, salt, cheese, meat extract cubes   2 lb   6½ oz
Water, two pints   2 lb   8 oz

One should not, however, jump to the conclusion that all soldiers carried the same weight at all times. Early assaults were indeed sometimes carried out with the kit as described above, but even in 1914 a 'fighting equipment' order was recognised to be used at the discretion of the unit commander. When in fighting equipment the pack was discarded in exchange for two extra 50-round ammunition bandoleers, bringing down the overall weight by about 5 lb, but increasing the ammunition available to a very respectable 250

rounds. Photographic evidence from the early part of the war also suggests that some units at least marched, or were transported, without full equipment, but with the greatcoat worn in the form of a roll over the shoulder.

Soon after the outbreak of war, extra items were being added to a soldier's kit, wire cutters, new weapons, and steel helmets being only the most obvious. On the other hand, even by the time of the first day on the Somme, most troops had their kit as carried in battle reduced. Main packs were now often left behind as a matter of course, but items such as sand bags, grenades and signal flags were carried instead. Battle weight therefore varied considerably with time and place, details of the load often being decided at brigade or even battalion level. Very often different 'waves' of the same assault would carry different loads, first and second lines might concentrate on weapon carrying capacity, whilst subsequent echelons might be more heavily burdened with bombs, bullets and trench mortar rounds for

Above.

Officer's personal equipment. Foreground is an issue marching compass by Short and Mason Limited of London 1915; the leather carrying case with which it is associated is dated 1914, and is by J.A. Jacobs and Company. In the centre of the picture are a pair of artillery officer's private purchase field glasses, virtually identical to the 'Binocular Mark V' as illustrated in the *Handbook of Artillery Instruments* of 1914. The long object in a leather carrying case at the back of the picture is a private purchase officer's glass drinking flask by Webb and Son of Plymouth; a stamp suggests that it was carried by an officer of the Royal Scots. It comes complete with a small drinking cup. The pistol is an issue Very single shot flare gun, by Webley and Scott Limited, dated 1915. M.S.

Right.

Tools of the trenches. Seen here are two versions of the wire cutters, both manufactured by Chater Lea Limited. The smaller pair fold down for storage in a handy webbing frog which bears Mills Equipment company marks and the date 1917. The folding 'trench saw' in its brown leather case consists of a flexible 'snake' of cutting teeth, through holes at either end of which are inserted wooden peg handles. The other two objects are periscopes: one takes the form of a small mirror with fold over metal cover which was simply attached to a bayonet or stick and held up over the parapet. G.C., M.S.

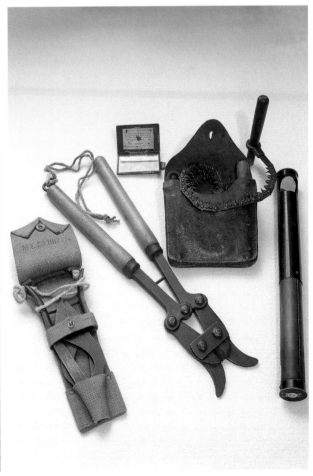

Above

Royal Engineers prepared for mounted duty wearing Pattern 1903 leather bandoleers. Several wear breeches, and the corporal also wears spurs. The man to the right of the group has leather leggings and a 1914 Pattern winter cap.

Left.

A private of the Loyal North Lancashires, c. 1914, wearing the Pattern 1908 webbing in the configuration originally intended with the main pack on the back and the haversack at the hip.

resupply, food, and even digging equipment and tools to reinforce the position. 'Average' or 'standard' load therefore became more and more meaningless as a concept. A man on sentry duty in a quiet sector might carry under 30 lb, being merely the clothes he stood up in, a rifle and a little ammunition: conversely an ammunition carrier for a trench mortar moving up in a support wave after an attack might have 80 lb or more of impedimenta. By 1917, manuals were recommending that 'assaulting troops should be as lightly equipped as possible', but it was not always advice that was heeded.

An interesting example of the possible variation in loads is provided by operational orders to the battalions of 55th Division, issued prior to the attack

Men of the King's Own (Royal Lancaster Regiment) pictured wearing white buff leather Slade Wallace equipment. This kit was replaced with the Pattern 1908 webbing, but continued to be seen on the parade ground for ceremonial duties for some time afterwards.

at the Third Ypres in 1917. These documents specified that the troops were to advance in 'fighting order with packs'; the majority of the riflemen carrying 200 rounds of ammunition. Specialists like signallers, Lewis gunners and bombers carried only 50 rounds of ammunition but were burdened with other weapons and equipment instead. Rifle grenadiers carried no ammunition pouches, but took their few cartridges in a bandolier. Each company received 16 pairs of wire cutters, and any man carrying particularly heavy equipment was permitted to leave his entrenching tool behind. Into every pack was to go rations; ground sheet; mess tin; spare water bottle of 'cold tea without milk or sugar'; holdall; soap; towel and oil tin. Additionally every man was expected to carry two grenades and a flare in his jacket pockets, and three spare sand bags tucked under the pack straps.

What was worn by the mass of units who garrisoned the trenches when no attack was in progress was different again. General instructions contained in *Notes For Infantry Officers*, c. 1917, stated that 'All men in the fire trenches, and a proportion of men in the support trench, will wear all their equipment (except packs) at all times.' Working parties were to be allowed to remove their equipment, but were supposed to keep it close at hand.

By August 1914 the regulars had been fully kitted out with the new Pattern 1908 webbing, but there were insufficient stocks to deal with the huge expansion of the army, leading to the adoption of other equipment. The main alternative was introduced in the *List of Changes* on 30 August 1914, and subsequently known as the 'Pattern 1914 leather equipment': this may have appeared similar in general outline to the 1908 web, but in many details it was inferior. Leather proved more difficult to handle in wet conditions, and more prone to deterioration. Instead of several small 'carriers' the 1914 set had just one large pouch on either side; these were clumsier, fitted less well to the body, and helped unbalance the equipment which in any case was said to bear down more on the hips than the web set. Moreover the two pouches accommodated only 60 rounds each, so that unless extra cartridges were carried elsewhere total capacity was only 120 rounds. Nevertheless a million or more sets of the leather and brass riveted 1914

Troops of the 18th Hussars shelter by a bank near Courcelles, 21 August 1918. This picture provides graphic evidence of the sort of burden the cavalry horse could be expected to bear including tack, weapons, feed bags, spare horse shoes, shovels and other sundries as well as the man and his equipment. The regimental brand mark '18H' can be identified on the rump of the animal nearest the camera. IWM Q 6973.

Pattern equipment were ordered, much of it going directly to Territorial and New Army battalions. It was also true that some sets of the 1914 Pattern general type were ordered directly by local committees rather than through the War Office, this may help to explain at least some of the minor variations encountered.

The 1914 Pattern equipment may have been intended as an interim measure, but even so it was frequently to be seen on active service in the trenches. Originally it was stated that the 1914 Pattern equipments should be 'stained as near as possible to the colour of the Service Dress', but in the event this requirement was swiftly dropped, and the colour was changed to a more natural looking 'London Brown'. The leather equipment worked as a stop gap but never proved popular, and troops often exchanged it for webbing when the opportunity arose.

A *General Routine Order* dated 12 December 1914

instructed infantry officers to adopt the same webbing as their men, taking where possible the equipment of wounded soldiers. This laudable idea, which would have helped them avoid sniper's bullets, was in fact often ignored, and photographs show that most officers continued to wear the old leather Sam Browne. The pattern current was that sealed in 1900, which was of brown 'bridle leather' and had a waist belt with straps over both shoulders, crossing at the back. From it were suspended a sword frog, pistol case and ammunition pouch. Many officers did indeed wear the two shoulder strap Sam Browne, but again strict regulation was flouted and a single shoulder strap worn across the chest proved more popular.

Officers' valises were supposed to be carried in transport, but this still left them with a considerable burden if their personal kit was made up according to the standard set down in the *Field Service Pocket Book* of 1914. A dismounted officer's impedimenta for example was supposed to weigh 42 lb 14 oz, of which 12 lb 6½ ozs accounted for by Service Dress, boots, underclothing, cap, braces and identity discs. About 6 lb 2½ oz of the total weight was in rations and water. The remainder was intended to be made up of the following:

Above.
Royal Artillery personnel load a Lewis gun and ammunition onto a motor cycle combination. The three men on the right all wear the leather jerkin. The man on the left is equipped for mounted duty, with bandoleer and various items like the water bottle and haversack dangling below waist level, plus a pair of sheepskin gloves and a stick.

Right.
An officer's brown leather field or trench boots, pictured with a stone ware rum jar stamped with the three letters 'S.R.D.'. This actually stood for 'Supply Reserve Depot' but was reinterpreted by the Tommies as 'seldom reaches destination' or 'service rum diluted'. M.S.

Field Service Pocket book		10 ozs
Cap, comforter (carried in greatcoat pocket)		3½ ozs
Compass, in case		4 ozs
Wire cutters	1 lb	4 ozs
Field dressing, in skirt of jacket		2 ozs
Binoculars or telescope	2 lb	
Greatcoat	7 lb	1½ ozs
Handkerchief		2 ozs
Clasp knife with ring and swivel		6 ozs
Map		2 ozs
Matches		1 oz

Private R. Ogden, No. 1 Ammunition Park, B.E.F.—"I have ridden two prominent makes, but the little 'Douglas' wipes the map with them all. There is not a better machine for hard work."

Private R. Ogden of Number one Ammunition Park riding a Douglas motor cycle, c.1915: note the special dispatch rider clothing of helmet, jacket and leggings. The Douglas company supplied no less than 25,000 motor cycles to the forces during the war, a figure second only to the 30,000 purchased from Triumph.

Watch and wrist strap		4 oz
Whistle and lanyard		2½ ozs
Sam Browne belt	2 lbs	
Greatcoat carrier		9 ozs
Haversack		11 ozs
Mess tin	1 lb	9 ozs
Sword knot		1½ ozs
Water bottle and sling		14 ozs
Pistol	1 lb	3 ozs
Sword	1 lb	2½ ozs
Scabbard		9½ ozs
Pistol ammunition		9½ ozs

Amongst these items were quite a few not officially carried by the other ranks in 1914, most notably the *Field Service Pocket Book*, compass, wire cutters, maps, matches, wrist watch, whistle and lanyard, pistol and 12 rounds of ammunition, though issue wire cutters for example became more common with all ranks as

Scottish cooks from a sergeants' mess wearing canvas fatigue jackets and 'dungaree' clothing. The word 'dungaree' originally referred to the coarse Indian calico from which overalls were made.

the war progressed. The officer's pistol was not of any specified pattern, but, officially speaking at least, choice was restricted to whatever would take government issue ammunition, so in practice most officers went for one of the marks of Webley service revolver in .455 inch calibre. Initially the Mark IV which had been introduced in 1899 predominated, alongside smaller numbers of the 1913 vintage Mark V. Later on they were both overtaken numerically by the Mark VI, which had a six inch barrel and was first introduced in May 1915. Other types of Webley like the 'Army' and 'Target' models were also in use, as was the extraordinary Webley Fosberry, the barrel of which recoiled and recocked the mechanism between shots. Even so Smith and Wessons, Colts and various sorts of semi automatic were all carried as well. One unusual weapon actually seen in some quantity was the Spanish made 'Old Pattern' revolver, or 'O.P.' pistol, quantities of which had been bought in to make up for the shortfalls in supply. The pistol ammunition was carried in a small pouch on the waist belt, and some officers also carried 'speed loaders' like the Prideaux, which were small clips allowing all the chambers of the revolver cylinder to be loaded simultaneously, rather than one at a time. Another oddity sometimes seen in use with the Webley later in the war was the Pritchard-Greener bayonet, effectively a dagger which attached to the pistol; but it was probably no more effective than carrying a separate trench knife and so never appeared in great numbers.

Also specified for the officers' personal equipment were the binoculars or telescope; or indeed both if they could be carried in the same case. The army had begun to issue modern prismatic binoculars to artillery batteries and signallers from 1907 onwards, but surviving examples and modern research suggest that as a result of shortages a wide variety of patterns of many different origins were actually carried during the war by both officers and other ranks. Some of the oldest still in use were the Galilean models Mark IV and Mark V which dated back to the turn of the century and were theoretically rendered obsolete in 1911. Rather more up to date were the prismatic models 'No. 2' and 'No. 3', which were officially accepted in 1909 and 1911 respectively and featured in the *Handbook of Artillery Instruments* of 1914. Here they were illustrated with a rain guard, and a leather tab which was supposed to be fastened to a button on

the uniform to stop them banging against the wearer's chest. It is dubious, however, as to whether either of these features actually caught on as they were swiftly abolished and seldom if ever appear on contemporary photographs. All these British issue glasses had their private purchase commercial equivalents.

A number of foreign patterns of field glass were also in use. Samples of 'Bausch and Lomb' and 'Crown' American binoculars were bought in during 1915 and 1916, and perhaps 10,000 sets of French glasses were obtained through the Ministère de la Guerre in the last 18 months of the war. Most extraordinarily of all, an approach was made in Switzerland for optics which almost led to purchases of German glasses. Another illustration of desperate shortage was an appeal to the public launched by Field Marshal Lord Roberts just after the outbreak of war; this eventually netted over 14,000 pairs of binoculars of various types.

Private purchase trench periscopes were also particularly popular with officers. A number of different types occur in regimental collections, photographs and contemporary advertising. One of the most popular was the tube periscope, which as its

Fatigue dress, Service Dress, and cooks clothing as seen outside a Territorial artillery cookhouse.

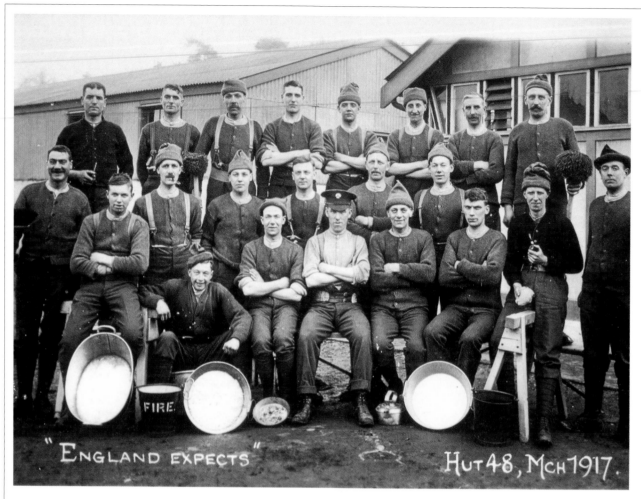

"ENGLAND EXPECTS"

FIRE.

HUT 48, MCH 1917.

Grenadier Guards in camp, March 1917. Amongst the items of clothing worn are no less than three variations on the cardigan, 'caps, comforter', and grey collarless shirts.

name suggests was a relatively unobtrusive metal tube in which were set the necessary mirrors. In some examples the tube was itself telescopic, collapsing down vertically into a handy shape for carriage. Other tube periscopes lacked this refinement, but were fitted with a wooden handle, making them more convenient to use without exposing the viewer's hands over the parapet. Another popular pocket model contained two small rectangular mirrors joined by a scissor-like lattice work of metal struts which could be opened out to a sufficient height to see over the top. A good example of one such periscope bearing the brand name 'Life Guard Pocket Periscope', contained in a khaki drill cover, is on display in the museum of the Sherwood Foresters at Nottingham Castle. Perhaps the simplest of all the private purchase periscopes was the mirror with a spring clip on the back which the user attached to a bayonet or stick. This type had the advantage of being very easy to carry and store, but the disadvantage that the user had to turn his back on the enemy in order to observe them.

Officers often carried waterbottles, sometimes the

issue type as used by the men, but there were numerous other possibilities. The recommended pattern from the 1911 regulations was of aluminium, slightly kidney shaped to fit the body, and with a cork stopper attached by a short chain. It was felt covered, held in a carrier, and worn suspended by means of a brown leather strap. A number of surviving examples, including one on display in the museum of the Duke of Lancaster's Own Yeomanry, show that this recommendation was indeed followed. Another private purchase type sometimes seen was in the form of an elongated glass flask, with a hinged closure and a small cup over the top. This was carried in a brown leather cover with a strap.

Swords, which appear to have been widely carried by officers in August 1914, seem pretty rapidly to have joined the baggage. Even so most officers did possess a blade, for to be given or to buy one was part of the ritual of commissioning which set the officer apart from the 'other rank', and swords were still to be seen on the parade ground even when Service Dress was worn. The standard infantry officer's sword, as approved in 1902, was described in the 1911 *Dress Regulations* as having a blade 32 inches and 9/16ths in length, a nickel plated steel guard, and a wooden grip covered in fish skin bound with silver wire. It was held

Army Service Corps personnel pose with their General Service wagons and other tools of the trade. Also notable are the varying patterns of shirt and the broad stable belts with multiple buckles.

in a nickel plated steel scabbard for ceremonial purposes, but for field service the scabbard was of brown leather covered wood. The hilt of the sword was decorated with a knot ending in an 'acorn', the original purpose of which had been to secure the sword to the wrist during combat. In field service the knot was brown leather, black being used by rifle units. The sword guard was decorated with the Royal Cypher (with strung bugle on the rifle pattern), and often the blade bore decorative etching. It is notable that at least a proportion of those swords carried by officers in 1914 had khaki cloth covers over the guard: a well provenanced example of this practice is preserved in the museum of the Royal Warwickshires at St. John's House, Warwick. Contrary to strict regulation, officer's swords sometimes bore personal inscriptions, most usually initials or family crests.

There were other minor unit variations and special versions for senior officers, but perhaps the most dramatically different of the officers' swords was the 'Claymore, Officer's, Highland Pattern' which had

first been approved in 1863. Properly speaking the Highland officer's sword was not really a Claymore at all but a basket hilted broadsword. It was carried in a steel scabbard, and again, at least in theory, the form of the blade was subject to strict regulation. In practice there were a number of regimental variations, and sometimes old family blades were carried.

The standard personal equipment of the mounted troops in 1914 was the Pattern 1903 bandoleer equipment, which, strangely enough, had also seen service as infantry equipment when first introduced. By virtue of the fact that the horse was expected to carry the majority of the load, the cavalryman, at least initially, got away with relatively little weight actually attached to his person. As the name suggests the main element of the 1903 equipment was the bandoleer, a broad strap of leather worn across the shoulder on which there were ammunition pouches closed by flaps. This arrangement seems to have been a direct result of early experience in the Boer War, where a combination of long distance marches, rough terrain, open topped cavalry bandoleers and large infantry pouches had sometimes led to a trail of dropped cartridges across the veldt. First models of the Pattern 1903 bandoleer apparently had five pouches with ten rounds in each, but later an extra four pouches were

Men of a Royal Engineers pigeon section pose for a photo in cold weather. Several wear 'mounted' great coats but the man in the centre wears a waistcoat of both light and dark fur.
Lancashire Museums.

added bringing the ammunition capacity up to a rather more respectable 90 rounds. During the war it became normal for each cavalryman to have two such bandoleers, one worn by himself, the other around the neck of the horse, so that a mounted man had 180 shots immediately available. The bandoleer was usually teamed with a web haversack (of either standard 1908, or slightly modified 1911 'other services' type), great coat straps, a web or a leather waist belt and a water bottle. Perhaps the greatest drawback to the cavalryman's personal equipment was that although it was designed to be most useful when on the back of a horse, in the Great War the cavalry spent much of their time on foot well away from the horse lines. Adding to the equipment for prolonged dismounted use was therefore the work of necessity rather than part of a carefully preplanned system.

On the cavalry horse itself was often stowed a considerable burden of impedimenta. This would typically include not only the saddle itself, usually of either 1912 universal type or 1890 'modified' Pattern,

but horse shoe cases, a frog for the Pattern 1908 cavalry troopers sword, feed bags, and a leather 'bucket' for the rifle. Two such patterns of 'Bucket, Rifle' were mentioned in Lists of Changes as issued prior to the war, the Marks 'III' and 'IV'. The trooper's mess tin was stowed attached to the bucket. Saddlery and horse furniture alone weighed 44 lb 12 oz. Special horse furniture was also devised to allow the carriage of various types of machine gun on the horse's back. Total weight of equipment carried as standard in 1914, both on the mounted man and the horse, amounted to a grand total of 251 lb 12 oz, or about 18 stone. If the soldier himself was taken into account this suggests that the horse carried a load of about 30 stone.

A group of Territorials from the King's Own (Royal Lancaster Regiment) in October 1914, two of whom are still wearing the Pattern 1903 bandoleer equipment. By this time the bandoleer was usually worn by the cavalry.

Right.
Irish Guardsmen tending a wounded German in a trench during the battle for Pilkem Ridge, 31 July 1917. The stretcher bearer nearest the camera is wearing his steel helmet back to front, revealing a carelessly hung chain mail visor. Note that the Guardsmen wear cloth regimental titles at the tops of their sleeves. IWM Q 2628

Khaki Drill

Though the vast majority of British troops served on the Western Front there was a significant presence in Mesopotamia, Palestine, Italy, Gallipoli, Greece, parts of Africa and elsewhere. Egypt and India both maintained substantial garrisons. For 'stations abroad' in warm climates the prescribed dress of the soldier was the Khaki Drill uniform, comprising a cotton 'frock' and trousers. According to the 1914 *Clothing Regulations* most troops including cavalry, infantry and artillery were entitled to three complete suits of such clothing in warm climes whilst Royal Engineers and mechanics, whose duties rendered them even more prone to getting dirty, warranted four sets. Interestingly 'non Europeans' often received the same clothing but in less generous allocations.

The Khaki Drill or 'K.D.' uniform was lighter in weight, cooler, and was coloured a dusty or light brown compared to the heavy and more deeply coloured serge Service Dress. Nevertheless the general shape of the garments was similar. The Khaki Drill frock fastened up the front with five buttons, had breast pockets which were closed with a flap and button, shoulder straps, and cuffs which were usually pointed. Although it seems that the standard type of jacket was that with a stand and fall collar there is photographic evidence to show that obsolete garments with a small stand up collars were also used. The trousers were long and intended for wear with boots and puttees, though behind the line canvas shoes were worn on certain occasions. Shorts were also very widely used, though not specifically mentioned in the 1914 Regulations. A curious and probably unofficial modification to the issue trousers sometimes seen was the cutting of slits up the sides as far as the knee and the addition of buttons, which allowed the legwear to be worn buttoned up as shorts, or let down as long trousers.

Officers' 'K.D.' jackets were loose fitting, fastened with four buttons, had four pockets and shoulder straps, and were open at the neck showing the shirt and tie. They thus followed the pattern of the usual Service Dress as laid down in *Dress Regulations*. However, rank badges were worn in metal at the shoulder, and the jacket cuffs were pointed. Photographic evidence suggests that the only gorget patches seen on a regular basis were the red tabs of Staff and General Officers. With the jacket, officers could wear khaki drill trousers, or breeches with leggings.

Probably the most interesting feature of the uniform for warm climates was the headgear. Though certain non-European troops were supplied with turbans, and even the fez, the regulation hat for British troops was the Wolseley Pattern helmet. Pre-war this was supplied to the troops one per man, complete with two 'Pagris' or decorative windings, chin strap, cover, badge and bag. The Wolseley Pattern, variously described as a 'solar topee', 'pith hat', 'Foreign Service Helmet' or even 'Bombay Bowler', was a light rigid headgear externally clad in sewn Khaki Drill panels. It was of dubious utility, but being broader and longer than earlier models did at least keep the sun off the head, face and neck. Protection of the neck could be further improved by the addition of the curtain sometimes seen in photographs. The officers' Wolseley was listed under the heading 'Helmet, Universal, Foreign Service' in the *Dress Regulations*, and described as: 'cork, made with six seams; bound with buff leather; projecting brim all round, 3 inches front, 4 inches back, 2 inches at sides; ventilated at the top . . . side hooks. . [and a] Brown leather chin strap 3/8 inch wide.'

Although pre-war regulations mention 'badges', many photographs of 1914 show the Wolseley with no embellishments or additions whatsoever. Moreover within a year or two, many units were sporting a bewildering variety of flashes and patches. These distinctions appear to have been of two major types, regimental and divisional. As yet no comprehensive study has yet been made, though the Imperial War

2ND/23RD (COUNTY OF LONDON) BN. THE LONDON REGIMENT, 1916

1ST/9TH BN. THE DUKE OF CAMBRIDGE'S OWN (MIDDLESEX REGT.), 1918

2ND/19TH (COUNTY OF LONDON) BN. THE LONDON REGT. (ST. PANCRAS) 1917

Cigarette card illustration showing a London Regiment Territorial serving in Macedonia, 1916. The uniform comprises the normal Service Dress jacket with K.D. shorts, Wolseley Pattern helmet and 1914 Pattern leather equipment.

Cigarette card illustration of a Middlesex Regiment Territorial at Baghdad, 1918. Though he seems far too neat, the K.D. uniform with shorts and helmet with flash appear accurate enough.

Cigarette card illustration of a London Regiment Territorial as he might have appeared at the surrender of Jerusalem, December 1917.

Museum does contain the returns of a survey of such matters, and many individual regimental museums have details or examples relating to one or more of their battalions. In many instances units simply took their regimental colours and applied them in various permutations to circles, squares, diamonds and other geometrical shapes. Some battalions applied their titles in words or numbers to a red or grey ground, and it has been reasonably suggested that these represent a judicious recycling of old full dress uniforms. Some made use of brass shoulder titles for a similar purpose. In other cases regimental identification took the form of a stripe within the pagri. Examples have also been found of the application of divisional signs to Wolseley helmets with brigades being distinguished by different combinations of the same colours. Some interesting examples of these practices are as follows:

Unit	Patch or flash on Wolseley helmet
Shropshire Yeomanry	Dark blue square with red line from top left to bottom right.
Welsh Horse	Black vertical oblong with a Welsh leek and the letters 'W.H.' in white.
Norfolks (2nd Bn)	Yellow vertical oblong, central black stripe.
Suffolks (no specific battalion)	Pagri tied to cross over on left side of helmet, yellow flash shaped like a three towered castle.

Above.
Jam Tin bomb making at Gallipoli, 1915. Serge Service Dress trousers are worn but shirt sleeves, rope soled canvas shoes and a slouch hat are minor concessions to the climate. Note the explosive containers and the lengths of barbed wire being cut down to make lethal shrapnel. IWM Q 13281.

Left.
General Sir Edmund Allenby, right, with General Baillout at Ismailia. Allenby wears officers' K.D. with scarlet tabs and rank badges on the shoulder, staff arm band, breeches and leggings.

Royal Sussex (1st Bn)   Red rectangle with words 'ROYAL SUSSEX' in white.

Royal Sussex (1/4th Bn)   Royal blue with dark blue vertical stripe.

Royal Sussex (1/5th Bn)   Orange and blue rectangles on a grey ground.

Royal Sussex (16th Yeo. Bn)
                          Diamond, yellow over blue.

The 'mix and match' approach to Service Dress and Khaki Drill as demonstrated in a photographers studio, Jerusalem, 3 July 1918. Here a serge Service Dress jacket is teamed with K.D. shorts, and as befits a mounted man, puttees tied at the ankle. Though obviously posed there cannot have been much preparation for this picture as is indicated by the filthy boots.

Brigadier C.L. Smith V.C., commanding officer of the Camel Brigade in the Sinai - Palestine campaign. Originally with 2nd Battalion the Duke of Cornwall's Light Infantry, Smith won his Victoria Cross in Somaliland in 1904. He is seen here in a tent wearing the K.D. uniform with scarlet gorget patches, a neck flap version of the K.D. cap, and carrying a fly whisk. 14th/20th King's Hussars.

Hampshires (1/4th Bn)	Rectangle, vertically bisected black and yellow.
Hampshires (2/4th Bn)	Initially black diamond with yellow quadrant within upper tip, later as 1/4th Bn.
Hampshires (1/5th Bn)	Black square with '5 HANTS' embroidered in gold.
Hampshires (1/6th Bn)	Square, vertically bisected black and yellow.
Hampshires (1/7th Bn)	Square diagonally bisected; bottom right yellow, top left black.
Hampshires (2/7th Bn)	As 1/7th battalion above.

Hampshires (1/9th Bn)	Black rectangle '9 HAMPSHIRE' embroidered in gold.
Dorsets (battalion not given)	4th and 8th folds of the pagri in green.
South Lancashires (battalion not given)	Red, white, and blue vertical stripes.
Essex (4th Bn)	Circle vertically bisected black and red.
Essex (5th Bn)	Triangle vertically bisected black and red.

Essex (6th Bn)	Oblong vertically bisected black and red.
Essex (7th Bn)	Square vertically bisected black and red.
Middlesex (1/7th Bn)	Square vertically bisected red and yellow.
Middlesex (2/8th Bn)	Diamond horizontally bisected red over yellow.
Middlesex (1/9th Bn)	Rectangle vertically bisected red and yellow.
North Staffs (7th Bn)	Black diamond.
Highland Light Infantry (1/6th Bn)	Truncated cone shaped patch of Mackenzie tartan.
Kent Cyclist Bn	Black diamond with white horse and words 'INVICTA 1st KENT'.

T.E. Lawrence was not the only officer in the Middle East to 'go native'. Here Lieutenant Shibley poses in full Arab regalia at Bishara in 1918.

Duke of Lancaster's Own Yeomanry, Egypt and Palestine, 1916-1917.

The 138 officers and men of 'A' squadron Duke of Lancaster's Own Yeomanry were deployed to Egypt in September 1914. As part of 42nd (East Lancashire) Division they were initially placed in defence of the Suez Canal, taking part in mopping up operations after the failed Turkish attack of February 1915. Early the next year, the DLOY was redeployed to the Western Frontier Force to operate against the Senussi tribesmen. This little known but successful campaign was marked by lengthy marches across difficult terrain, without tents, and often with a blanket as the only shelter. In one four day period alone the unit covered 122 miles.

By July 1916, the squadron was on active service against the Turkish field force of German general Kress von Kressenstein, but after the battle of Romani the threat to the Canal was removed, and the British prepared for the offensive. As part of 53rd (Welsh) Division, and subsequently as a component of XXI Corps Cavalry Regiment, the DLOY took part in the advance into Palestine. Though disease and fatigue took a heavier toll than battle, the unit was involved in several sharp flights, and lost its second in command in the skirmish at Hesi Ridge.

The DLOY were equipped with Khaki drill uniform on arrival in Egypt. Regimental photograph albums show that the jackets were often worn with the brass shoulder title 'T' over 'Y' over 'D OR LANCASTER'S', but that helmet flashes were not adopted until late in the war. The reconstruction shows an officer, left, and two other ranks in action. The officer wears the 'K.D.' version of the Service Dress cap, but slouch hats and Wolseley Pattern helmets were also worn. He wears shoulder rank insignia; also cap and regimental collar badges, which include a garter, rose and ducal coronet motif. The revolver is retained by means of a lanyard around the officer's neck and the horse wears a fly fringe over its eyes.

The other mounted man has drawn his 1908 Pattern sword but is also armed with a SMLE rifle which is carried in a leather bucket. The horsemen are passing one of the squadron's four Hotchkiss light machine guns, which contemporary squadron records refer to as Hotchkiss Rifles. Though useful they were not with the unit long since they were not received until mid way through the war, and were later taken away together with a seven man detachment to form part of the complement of an armoured car unit. Painting by Christa Hook.

The Khaki Drill uniform at its simplest: Wolseley Pattern helmet, K.D. jacket with pointed cuff and pocket details, K.D. trousers, 1914 Pattern leather belt, and boots.

31st Division (Senior Brigade)
            Square, horizontally bisected white over red.

31st Division (Intermediate Brigade)
            Square, diagonally bisected upper left white, lower right red.

31st Division (Junior Brigade)
            Square, horizontally bisected red over white.

Even though the Wolseley was worn by a majority of British soldiers in hot theatres of war there were other forms of headgear in regular use. Officers often wore caps similar to the ordinary Service Dress cap but made out of 'K.D.' material, with or without neck flaps or curtains. Slouch hats, which were certainly not the sole prerogative of Australians and New Zealanders, were also seen in significant numbers on

A sergeant of a mounted unit ready to leave England to join 42nd (East Lancashire) Division in the Middle East. He wears the normal Service Dress with breeches, puttees, boots and spurs, and a Colt 'New Service' revolver in an open topped leather holster. The only concession yet made to the new climate is the presence of the Wolseley Pattern helmet.
Lancashire Museums.

British troops. Photographic evidence shows the slouch hat being worn in a variety of manners, sometimes with the brim down, sometimes with the left side turned up and held in place with a regimental badge.

Perhaps the most remarkable feature of the wearing of 'K.D.' overseas was the degree to which it was mixed with the normal Service Dress, or worn in part only. In Italy and in transit ordinary Service Dress was sometimes worn with the Wolseley helmet. Surviving photographs from Palestine, Greece and Mesopotamia show the uniforms being worn 'half and half', Service Dress jacket with Khaki Drill shorts. On other occasions whole battalions wore the slouch hat with Service Dress trousers and shirt, or shorts and shirt with Wolseley helmet. Though Highland troops, like other infantry, were issued with complete 'K.D.' uniforms certain battalions took to the field clad in kilt, shirt and Wolseley Pattern helmet.

Above.

Men of the Duke of Lancaster's Own larking about on the Nile, June 1915. Note the non-regulation shirt, identity disc and (reversed) Wolseley Pattern. DLOY collection.

Right.

An old campaigner in the Khaki Drill uniform, c. 1918, wearing three 'overseas' chevrons and three long service good conduct chevrons. Note also the wrist watch with protective cover.

Weapons

Rifle and Bayonet

In 1914, the great armies of the world all relied on the bolt action magazine rifle as their primary arm. Britain was no exception, and there was considerable emphasis on the regular soldier's speed and accuracy with this weapon. The standard rifle at the outbreak of war was the .303 in 'SMLE', or Short Magazine Lee Enfield, teamed with a Pattern 1907 bayonet. The SMLE was first approved and announced in the *List of Changes* on 23 December 1902, its introduction having been at least in part precipitated by the experience of the Boer War, where the desirability of a rifle combining the best features of the old 'Long', or Magazine Lee Enfield (MLE) with a shorter barrel to create a 'universal' arm for both cavalry and infantry was first realised. By 1914 minor alterations had produced the SMLE Mark III.

Though the relatively short barrel of the SMLE gave rise to a fairly harsh recoil with the latest Mark VII ammunition, and despite the fact that the Mauser action may have been fractionally more accurate at long ranges, the SMLE was a compromise which actually worked superbly. It would remain as the British soldier's main arm, with only minor

Line drawing of the Short Magazine Lee Enfield, (Mark III) and bayonet as depicted in the *Musketry Regulations*.

modification, for over 50 years and though by then distinctly superannuated would survive in other forms and other countries for upwards of 80 years. Amongst its desirable features were a ten-round magazine, when many other countries including Germany had rifles with only a five-round capacity, a moderate length, a reliable action, and a short bolt pull. This last feature was useful in that it allowed a soldier to keep his eyes, and the rifle, on target whilst loading, and aided swiftness of operation. A rate of fire of 15 rounds a minute was the claim of the veterans of Mons, and this was by no means an idle boast. Tests at Hythe in 1912 had pitted the SMLE against the German service rifle in speed trials: in expert hands with unlimited supplies of ammunition the German rifle could manage 15 rounds a minute; the Lee Enfield could be pushed to 28. Moreover, British training, as expounded at Hythe and printed in the *Musketry Regulations* of 1909, stressed not only accuracy but 'volume' of fire, as well as the usefulness of short, rapid fusillades.

The SMLE was a 'charger loading' weapon. This meant that its ammunition came in small chargers of five rounds, and was usually loaded by opening the bolt, placing a full charger in a guide above the magazine and pressing down the cartridges with the thumb. Two such chargers filled the magazine. To fire, the bolt was closed, automatically pushing any empty charger out of the way and leaving the mechanism

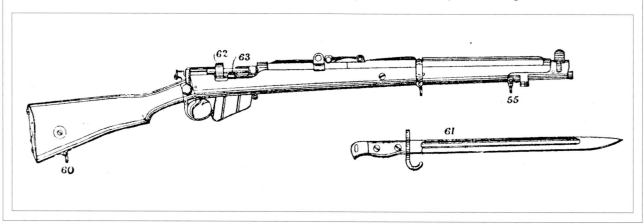

cocked, and then the trigger could be squeezed. The rifle was sighted to 2,000 yards, and could indeed kill at a mile, especially where bodies of men fired as a group in good weather at a very large target. Such circumstances scarcely if ever occurred on the Western Front, however, and the vast majority of targets were engaged at 400 yards or less. Even much sniping took place at as little as 100 to 200 yards.

The standard ammunition for active service was referred to by the old fashioned term 'ball', though in fact the lead projectiles were jacketed and sharply pointed. A round of 'ball' was powerful enough to penetrate up to nine inches of brick at close range. There were also blank cartridges and 'Cartridges, Small Arm, Dummy, Drill', for practice where real bullets were not required. The dummy cartridges were identifiable at a glance by virtue of the fact that they were steel rather than brass, or had holes drilled through them. Ammunition was usually delivered to the units in 1,000 round boxes, in which were 20 standard 50-round bandoleers. Apart from ammunition boxes and bandoleers another accessory frequently seen with the SMLE in the mud of trenches was the breech cover. Many were improvised from old socks or sacking, but from January 1915 there were also semi official versions ordered locally in

Detail of two examples of the S.M.L.E. seen together with the 50 round cotton bandoleer and an issue breech cover. Ink stampings indicate that this Mark II bandoleer was made by Hampton's in June 1916. Notice the three stud closure of the breech cover and the leather thong, which, though seen tied around the cover in this instance, was often attached to the rifle by means of the small ring just in front of the magazine. When thus secured the cover could be torn off quickly but not lost. G.C., M.S.

France by Divisional Ordnance Officers. Any waterproof material was admissible, so long as the finished item 'cost not exceeding one franc'. Finally, in June 1915, a genuine issue cover was introduced, the 'Cover, breech, Mark I'; this was made of double texture waterproofed drill and fitted with three press stud buttons. Wire cutters of several patterns were also made to fit onto the end of the rifle; some appear to have been bladed, but more usually they simply acted as a guide, drawing the wire in front of the muzzle where it was severed with a round from the rifle. The system was not apparently a huge success, and seems to have been largely discontinued after the war.

The pre-war SMLE was well finished and, counting the oil bottle stored in the butt, consisted of

A Territorial of the South Lancashires demonstrates the use of a periscope rifle in the trenches near Bois Quarante, 1915. Periscope rifles, or 'hyposcopes' made an early appearance in the war as they seemed to offer a way to shoot without fear of retaliation. There were several different models, both improvised and official, and patents for both French and English types were taken out during the war. A General Routine Order allowed the issue of eight Espitallier Sniper scopes per battalion. As can be seen here, most models consisted of a rifle; a mechanism by means of which it could be remotely operated, and a periscope. Queen's Lancashire Regiment.

about 70 machined components. It was also used by Empire forces, though initially not by the Canadians who opted for the unreliable Ross. It was no wonder, therefore, that demand for the rifle soon outpaced supply, and that the result was a simplification of the original SMLE Mark III, which deleted the original long range sights, windage adjustment and magazine cut off. This slightly simplified rifle was introduced in January 1916 as the Short, Magazine Lee Enfield, Mark III *. Several other weapons were to be seen in the hands of the troops during the war. Foremost amongst these were the old MLEs, longer and less handy than the newer short rifle, but nevertheless serviceable, and sufficiently similar to require little or no extra training.

Also seen in significant numbers were the Pattern 1914 Enfields. These had a convoluted history in that prior to the war a change to a .276 inch rifle of higher than normal velocity had been envisaged. Plans had been prepared and trials made in 1913, but in the event war came suddenly and the project was shelved due to the problems inherent in introducing a new service cartridge at such a critical moment. As a result of shortages it was decided to complete the new rifle in .303 inch calibre and it was made in the U.S. by contractors including Remington and Winchester for British service. The P14 was totally unlike the Lee Enfields of old, having a Mauser type action and a five-round magazine. It may not have been quite as swift as the SMLE but soon gained a reputation for accuracy, becoming an efficient target and sniper rifle. Whilst the Long Enfields and the P14 made acceptable stop gaps and were frequently seen in the front line, there were other guns which probably should never have been bought in the first place. One such was the Japanese Arisaka rifle, introduced to British forces in February 1915 as the 'Rifle, Magazine, .256 inch, Pattern 1900', another was the Canadian Ross, which though it possessed a very

Above.

The winners of the inter platoon challenge cup, 6th Knutsford Battalion, Cheshire Volunteer Regiment, pose with their trophy and American made P14 rifles. Many Volunteer units were formed in 1914, being officially recognised and placed under the control of the Central Association of Volunteer Training Corps. Though not strictly part of the Regular Army, these units often wore similar uniform and formed a valuable pool of partially trained manpower. In April 1916, the Volunteers were renamed the Volunteer Force, had their badges of rank altered to conform with the regulars, and were instructed to wear the Royal Arms cap badge seen here. By the end of the war, plans were in train to make Volunteer battalions part of the line regiments.

Right.

The Boer War vintage Magazine Lee Enfield seen in the hand of a Territorial of the Rifle Brigade, about November 1915. Note the Pattern 1914 leather equipment and the Imperial Service badge worn over the right breast pocket.

elegant 'straight pull' bolt action, was pretty hopeless in mud and during lengthy rapid fire. Perhaps fortunately British troops did not have to take these to the trenches, and they served elsewhere in training thereby freeing better rifles for the front.

Whatever the rifle the weapon system was incomplete without a bayonet, for pre-war theory saw the 'fire fight', though very important, as only the first stage in a battle which would ultimately result in the infantry rushing forward to take up the ground, and if necessary engage in close combat with the enemy. Bayonet drill moreover was seen as a morale raising exercise which would inculcate aggressive spirit. Individual commanders and trainers varied as to their opinion of its usefulness, but even though edged weapon wounds counted for but a fraction of one per cent of the total, bayonets and bayonet drill remained. The Pattern 1907 bayonet which fitted to the muzzle of the SMLE by means of a ring and spring clip was originally made with a long hooked cross piece or 'quillon' on one side. This was deleted in October 1913, but both variations were seen in action. The 1907 types had a 17 inch blade, thus living up to their descriptions as 'sword' bayonets, and having sufficient length to give the bayonet fighter decent reach. Though not very useful much of the time there was little that could go wrong with the humble sidearm, and apart from detailed modifications to the scabbard,

A Smith and Wesson .455 inch revolver. The presentation inscription shows that it was given to a new officer on his promotion from the ranks in January 1917.

Opposite.
Top.
A selection of the weapons of trench warfare. The SMLE rifles, top and bottom, are fitted respectively with a 'No 3' Hale rifle grenade, and the 1907 Pattern bayonet. In the centre of the picture is a push dagger made by Robbins of Dudley. The two revolvers are a Webley Mark VI with a lanyard fitted, and a pre-war private purchase Webley 'W.G.' Army Model.

Bottom.
The Colt 'New Service' .455 inch revolver; just one of several American pistols which were imported to make up the shortages experienced by the British Army.

the only significant change to be instituted was the drilling of a small 'clearance hole' through the pommels from 1916 onward. These little holes were necessitated by the mud of the trenches, which, when caked in the bayonet's spring clip, prevented the catch from working. The bayonet for the P14 was similar in general outline to that of the SMLE, but the bayonets for the old MLEs were of the 1888 or 1903 type, and only 12 inches in length.

Many bayonets of all descriptions were altered by their users during the course of the war in an effort to produce practical trench knives for raiding and close combat. Most types were shortened, but the Ross

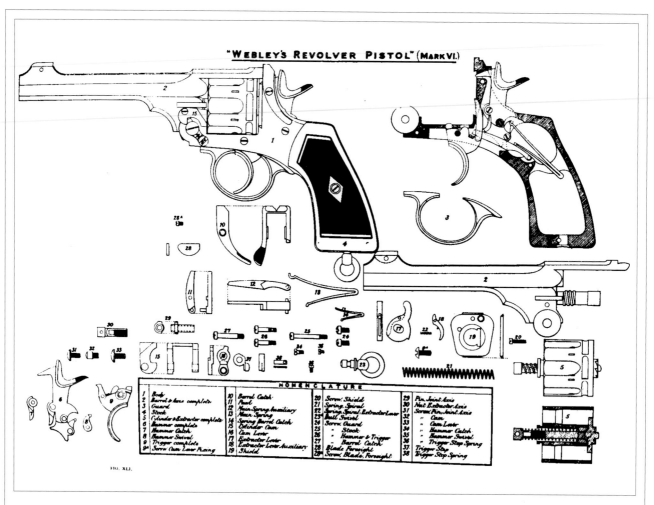

"WEBLEY'S REVOLVER PISTOL" (MARK VI.)

FIG. XLI.

Diagram showing the Webley Mark VI revolver and its parts.
This pistol would eventually become the commonest in
service.

bayonet, which already had something of the
silhouette of a combat knife about it, was a particular
favourite. Converted bayonets were therefore
common alongside various trench clubs, and the
specially made, and usually privately purchased, trench
knives. During the war, Robbins of Dudley became
particularly well known as a maker of trench knives,
and apart from their more conventional wares
produced 'push' daggers with their blades set at 90
degrees to the grip, for use with a thrusting motion.
Knuckle knives with guards around the outside of the
hand were also known, and apparently became
especially popular with the Americans. A particularly
outlandish combat knife was the 'Joubert' or 'Welsh'
knife, which looked like a fearsome if rather
impractical broad bladed short sword. It was used in
only limited numbers mainly by the Royal Welsh
Fusiliers.

Of probably greater significance than knives and
bayonets were the various equipments introduced
during the Great War to aid the sniper, though
officialdom was slow to recognise sniping as a separate

discipline, and its importance in trench warfare. At
first, most sniper equipments were private purchases
or improvisations. Officers who had been keen
stalkers before the war were the first to bring sporting
rifles to bear upon the enemy: amongst these weapons
were the Ross Model 1905, .280 inch rifle; the .416
Rigby and the high velocity Jeffreys .333 inch. Using
such weapons as these, some significant successes were
achieved, including Lieutenant L. Greener of the
Royal Warwickshire's tally of 54 Germans; yet in
general the enemy had the upper hand in the sniping
duels of 1914 and 1915. The problems were
compounded by a lack of optical equipment, the
market for which was dominated by German
manufacturers. Up to July 1915, just 1,260
government orders were placed for telescopic rifle
sights, most of them with the top London and
Birmingham gun makers, and these scopes were
expensive as well as scarce, costing between £6 and
£13 whilst the SMLE itself was only £3 10s. In
addition to the telescopic sights, 'magnifying' or
'Galilean' sights were also employed. These lacked the
tube of the telescopic sight proper, and consisted of a
convex and a concave lens attached individually to the
muzzle and breech of the gun. The four main types of
these sights were the Neill (also known as the Barnet

or Ulster); the Lattey; the Martin and Gibbs. Such equipment was prone to damage, had no cross hairs and a narrow field of view, but was relatively cheap at between 10s and £5 per set.

Only by 1916, and with considerable prompting from sniper enthusiasts like Major H. Hesketh-Pritchard, who helped to establish 1st Army Sniping School, was both official training and supply pushed forward. During that year sniper scopes fitted for the SMLE began to reach the front in significant quantities, and General Routine Orders allotted each division rifles with scopes at the scale of four per battalion, but even then many of those supplied were less than perfect for the task. One of the most serious defects was that the main type of scope then issued was not mounted centrally over the bore of the rifle, but offset to the left. The logic behind this was that off set scopes still allowed the rifle to be charger loaded, yet

Right.

A sergeant of the 20th Hussars carries not only two children but the regulation straight bladed 1908 Pattern sword on his saddle. 14th/20th King's Hussars.

Below.

The .303 inch Maxim, the predecessor of the Vickers which was still to be seen in 1914. Contemporary French postcard.

few and far between were the instances when a careful sniper would wish to engage in rapid fire. About 10,000 telescopic sights were eventually supplied for the SMLE. The P14 Enfield was also used as a sniper weapon in the final days of the war when many were fitted with Aldis telescopes. The complete assembly was actually known as the 'Rifle, Magazine, .303 in, Pattern 1914, Mark I * (W) T'; with the 'W' standing for Winchester, and the 'T' for telescope.

In training and organisational terms, sniping was allowed to develop as a branch of scouting. Each battalion eventually grew its own sniper section, officially eight men strong but in practice anything between a dozen and two dozen men. Sections of the front were allotted to sniper NCOs, whose duty it was to control that area, being directed by the Intelligence or Sniping officer.

Pistols and Swords

Some remarks have already been made on officers' swords and pistols in the section relating to personal equipment. These weapons were not, however, solely the province of officers, and did, in certain instances, have their issue equivalents. Pistols, for example, were regularly issued to machine gunners, military police, gas troops, tank crews and certain other specialists. They were usually carried in leather holsters, open or closed top, frequently on the basic belts of the 1914 Pattern leather equipment. At the commencement of the war, Royal Flying Corps observation aircraft were not generally fitted with machine guns, and so a variety of pistols, grenades and even shotguns were carried by pilots. Despite some quite imaginative pistol training, and handiness in the confines of trench and bunker, the weapon was seldom a great success, and was essentially a last resort.

Issue pistols were normally distinguishable on close examination by the presence of the government Broad Arrow, and very often by unit marks. Officers' arms, by contrast, were often inscribed with the name of a retailer, or perhaps the owner's name or initials, since these were essentially private property. The most commonly encountered issue pistol is undoubtedly the .455 in calibre Webley Mark VI, with its six inch barrel, but earlier marks of Webley, the Smith and Wesson, Colt 'New Service' and the Spanish 'Old Pattern' revolver are not uncommon. Less frequently encountered were a number of semi automatic types like the Colt Model 1911 in British service calibre, and the Webley semi automatic. This last was effective enough, and certainly packed a punch, but was boxy and inelegant to look at. Its main issue was to the Navy, but it also saw action with the RFC, and possibly also experimental use with the Royal Horse Artillery.

The only other ranks to carry swords as a matter of course were the cavalry, and the standard issue arm was the model 1908 sword. With a long straight blade, a slightly inclined grip, and a plain steel bowl guard, it was certainly lethal enough, at least in theory. When orders were received to proceed abroad in 1914, cavalry swords were duly sharpened. Sadly however, as with the lance, there were very few circumstances under which they could actually be used. Even so, and somewhat paradoxically since the British army was in the forefront of tank development, a significant reserve of cavalry was maintained through much of the war on the Western Front.

Vickers Limited.

Latest Model Light Automatic Rifle Calibre Gun, Mounted upon Adjustable Tripod.
Rate of fire 600 rounds per minute. Erith Works, Kent.

An advertisement produced by Vickers Limited showing the 'latest model light automatic rifle calibre gun mounted upon adjustable tripod. Rate of fire 600 rounds per minute. Erith works, Kent.'

Machine Guns

The British army had used various hand cranked Gatling and volley guns during the last third of the 19th century but it would be the mid 1880s before the advent of a fully automatic machine gun which would continue to fire without any external power source. The first examples of Maxim machine guns were purchased by the British government in 1887, and before long both the War Office and Volunteer units were conducting trials with the new weapons in .450 calibre. By 1893, models using the latest .303 inch round had been made, and from then on the machine gun became a regular feature of the battlefield. November 1912 saw the adoption by the army of the new Vickers .303 inch, machine gun, but even at the outbreak of war there were many older Maxim weapons still in service.

Though lighter than its predecessors, the Vickers was hefty and watercooled; the gun alone weighed 40 lb, the tripod another 50 lb. It was also encumbered with a water container, condenser tube and fabric ammunition belts, each of 250 rounds. Each gun cost over £200. Yet by the standards of the time the Vickers was capable of awesome power, emptying a belt in half a minute and creating bullet swept 'beaten zones' out to well over a mile. The Vickers also had advantages in terms of concealment and economy of manpower. The machine gun was thought to be worth 30 to 40 riflemen in terms of fire effect yet it occupied a frontage of only two yards, and whilst prolonged use gave rise to a plume of steam it could well remain concealed until it opened fire. Though more men were useful as ammunition carriers, it could quite happily be operated by a crew of two. Its fire was very concentrated, being steadied by the sheer mass of the equipment.

To load and fire the Vickers, the crew first set up the tripod and removed the locating pins; the gun was now placed atop the mount and the pins replaced. Next, a fresh belt of ammunition from the belt box was offered up to the feed block, and the brass tag of the belt was fed through to the other side and the cocking handle operated. With loading complete it now remained to flip up the rear sight, estimate range, and, holding the spade grips, operate the thumb trigger which was located between them. In cases of

Above.
Motor Machine Gunners demonstrate the use of a Vickers against aircraft from a motor cycle combination.

Right.
Trench layout from the middle period of the war showing typical locations of MG positions and snipers posts.

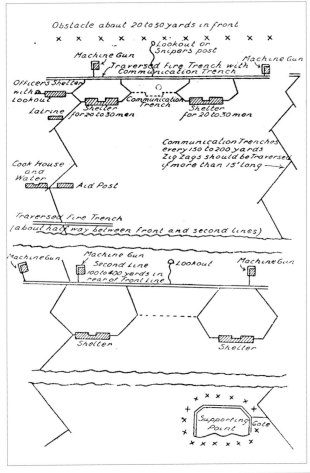

necessity, and with changes of barrel and top ups of water, a Vickers could plug away at 10,000 rounds per hour for several hours. Where this was not absolutely required it was more sensible to fire in short bursts and with frequent pauses, which not only conserved ammunition but kept the gun cooler, cut barrel wear, and allowed better observation of fire. It was generally recognised that three minutes of rapid fire would bring the water in the barrel casing to boiling. In defence, in static warfare, the 'MGs' or 'Emma Gees' as they were commonly known, were dug into their own special pits, and covered the front by means of interlocking zones, preferably so positioned that they were not at a right angle to the front but obliquely positioned for best fire effect and minimum exposure.

Effective though they were, what British machine guns in 1914 lacked was a thorough appreciation of their tactical worth, and the numbers to make a

Reconstruction of a Lewis gun ammunition carrier of the 8th Battalion Lancashire Fusiliers, 1918. On the shoulder and left arm are shown the 'LF' shoulder title, battalion number, lance corporal chevron and wound stripes. Notice also the Lewis gun webbing ammunition pouches, and the steel ammunition box with leather strap, dated 1918, which bears the legend 'Box Carriers Magazines Lewis .303 inch gun'. G.C., S.B.

Reconstruction detail showing the web equipment for carrying Lewis gun magazines. G.C., S.B.

decisive contribution. The BEF had only about 150 machine guns, or two per battalion in the front line at the start of the war. That this was far too few was quickly realised, yet it took time to double the number per battalion as the army itself was expanding so rapidly. Only a major industrial effort would put the situation to rights: between August and December 1914 only 266 Vickers guns were made; during 1915 production rose to 2,405, then in 1916 it went up to 7,429 units; 1917 saw 21,782 guns made. Finally in 1918, no less than 39,473 Vickers machine guns left the factories.

At the end of 1915, battalion Vickers machine guns were withdrawn from the infantry – who retained the new light machine guns – and brought together in companies of the new Machine Gun Corps. The companies of the Corps were so numbered that they agreed with the brigade to which they were attached.

Each MGC company consisted of about 200 men of which the fighting component was divided into four sections, each with its own officer. Each section had four guns, and six men for each gun. Finally in 1918, the machine gun companies were themselves grouped into Machine Gun Battalions. A new tactic frequently employed by the Machine Gun Corps was the machine gun barrage, groups of machine guns elevated to fire at distant targets, like cross roads and woods, and fired for set periods of time to deny them to the enemy. Such a fire mission might last several hours, and involve the expenditure of hundreds of thousands of rounds.

Perhaps the most important development in terms of the infantry in World War One was the advent of the light machine gun. Prior to the war there had been several experiments, both with semi automatic rifles and with machine guns which were light enough to be carried and if necessary operated by one man, but none had been adopted by the British army. The Belgians had, however, taken delivery of a handful of Lewis guns, and these rapidly showed their worth and soon attracted the attention of the hard pressed British.

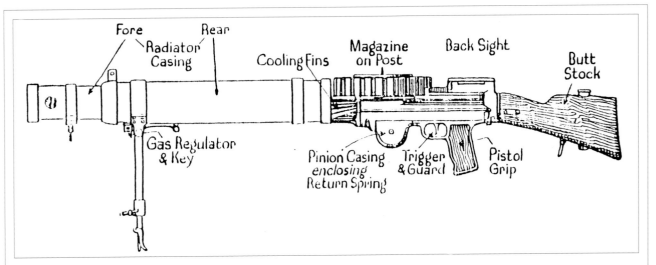

Diagram showing the main parts of the Lewis gun.

The precursor of the Lewis gun had been originally designed by the American Samuel Maclean, but was tripod mounted and had originally been intended as a competitor to guns like the Maxim. However, it was further developed and promoted by Maclean's countryman Colonel Isaac Lewis, thereby becoming a viable man portable weapon. As it finally appeared in British hands, it weighed 26 lb, and was fitted with an ammunition drum or pan for 47 rounds of .303 inch cartridges, and was sighted to 2,000 yards. Though still quite massive, considerable amounts of weight were saved by the fact that the gun was air cooled rather than watercooled, and that in place of a heavy tripod it usually made do with a light 'field mount' bipod. This arrangement had two important drawbacks. Firstly, air cooling was not as efficient, so long periods of sustained fire were not possible, and secondly, the light bipod and generally lower weight of the equipment meant that it was not as steady as the Vickers. It was therefore less accurate and could not be used so effectively at long range. Against these

A Lewis gunner wearing 1908 Pattern webbing poses in the prone firing position.

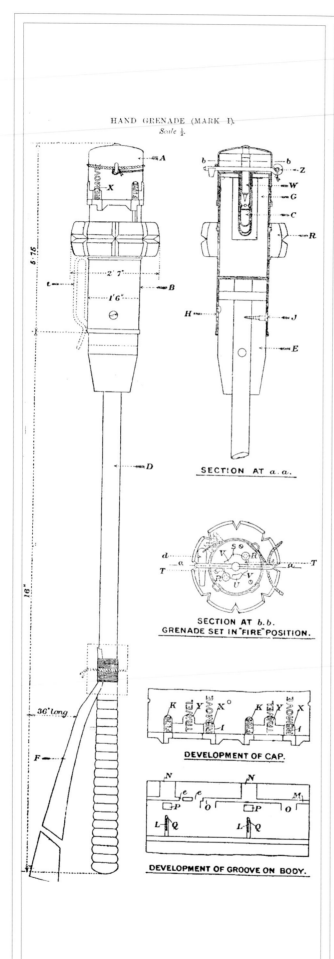

HAND GRENADE (MARK I).
Scale ½.

SECTION AT a.a.

SECTION AT b.b.
GRENADE SET IN "FIRE" POSITION.

DEVELOPMENT OF CAP.

DEVELOPMENT OF GROOVE ON BODY.

Left.

Diagram from the *Musketry Regulations* showing the Hand Grenade (Mark I) current in 1914.

Above.

The making of Jam Tin bombs behind the front line, c. 1914.

disadvantages had to be set the fact that a Lewis gun cost a fraction of the Vickers, could be carried substantial distances by one man, move and fire within moments, and was unimpeded by water cans and tubes. In short it helped to make possible a minor revolution in infantry tactics, and progressively the infantry companies and platoons were able to take with them their fire support wherever they went. Eventually the Lewis, combined with new grenades, rifle grenades and the rifle itself would make practical fire and movement of a very modern sort.

This was not achieved over night. It was July 1915 before there were sufficient Lewis guns for a general issue of four per battalion to begin, and the end of that year before a realistic target of one per platoon, or 16 per battalion could be set. By 1918, however, production reached 62,303 units, and during that year there were enough guns that two per platoon were allotted, which with an allowance of an extra four guns

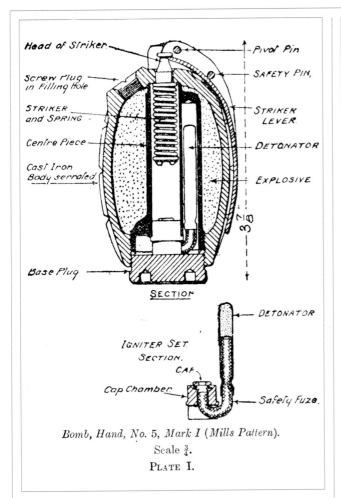

SECTION.

Head of Striker
Screw Plug in Filling Hole
Striker and Spring
Centre Piece
Cast Iron Body serrated
Base Plug

Pivot Pin
Safety Pin
Striker Lever
Detonator
Explosive

3⅜"

IGNITER SET. SECTION.

Detonator
Cap
Cap Chamber
Safety Fuze.

Bomb, Hand, No. 5, Mark I (Mills Pattern).
Scale ¾.
PLATE I.

Diagram of the mechanism of the 'No 5' Mills bomb.

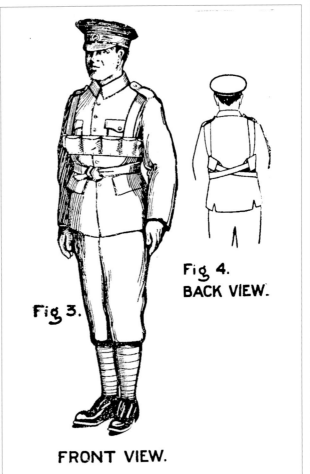

Fig 3.

Fig 4. BACK VIEW.

FRONT VIEW.

A sketch from a contemporary manual showing one of the earliest forms of waistcoat grenade carrier.

for anti-aircraft defence at HQ totalled no less that 36 Lewis guns per battalion. Thus it was that the Lewis first supplemented and then replaced the Vickers in the front line trenches and in the forefront of the attack, where the Germans soon learned to treat it with respect.

The Lewis brought with it a good deal of ancillary equipment which could materially alter the appearance of the soldier. There was a 'carrier' for four magazines, a web equipment with four circular pouches to accommodate eight magazines on the soldier's body, and a metal box with a leather strap, again capable of carrying eight magazines. For off battlefield transport, the Lewis could either be pushed or pulled in a small handcart, or moved by means of a horse drawn limber, which accommodated four guns, 176 filled magazines and 9,000 extra rounds. Another accessory was a robust sling, originally intended so that the gun did not have to be grasped when hot. Some put it to more aggressive use, actually utilising it to fire the Lewis from the hip. Such antics were hardly calculated to produce accurate fire, but were invaluable where no other mobile support was available. Trained Lewis gunners originally wore the same 'MG'

proficiency badge worn by the ordinary machine gunners, but by 1917 an 'LG' badge was in use.

One other machine gun which was in common use in British hands in the Great War was the French designed Hotchkiss light machine gun. Cavalry regiments had originally been issued with the Maxim, but weight, combined with the overwhelming demands of the infantry and later the Machine Gun Corps, led to the abandonment of tripod mounted watercooled weapons by the cavalry. From 1916 they had to rely on the Hotchkiss, which was a useful gun though arguably inferior to the Lewis. The Hotchkiss weighed 27 lb and fed from 30 round metallic strips. Its field mount was a small bipod. A modified gun, the Mark I *, was introduced in 1917; it was able to fire both from the strips and from a form of belt 50 rounds long. A diminutive tripod with all round traverse was also brought in, although, as with the Lewis, sustained fire was not its metier.

Grenades

As far as the grenade was concerned, Britain

A lead weighted, metal studded, wooden trench club surrounded by a Mills type 'No 23' hand and rifle grenade; a Battye hand grenade; a Hale rifle grenade; a caltrap designed to injure the feet of unwary horses and troops; and a Vickers machine gun belt, dated 1914. The two rounds of .303 inch ammunition show both the pointed bullet current during the war and the obsolete cartridge with round ended projectile.

S.B., M.S., Queen's Lancashire Regiment.

commenced the war lamentably ill equipped. Only the Royal Engineers were trained in the use of grenades, and only one bomb, the 'Grenade No 1', was on issue and that in tiny numbers. The No 1 which had entered service in 1908 was an outlandish piece of equipment, percussion ignited and mounted on a 16 inch cane throwing handle. A yard of streamer at the end of the cane was designed to ensure that it landed nose first. The grenade produced a satisfying enough explosion but was imperfect in many ways: it was expensive to manufacture, costing £1 1s 3d a time; had poor fragmentation characteristics; and, in the confined space of a trench, could be a liability to its user. A short handled version was soon devised, but grenade production lagged disastrously behind demand throughout 1914 and 1915.

The troops in France and Flanders were therefore quickly forced onto their own resources and improvised grenades were made at the front. The main two types were the 'hairbrush' or 'racket' bomb and the apparently more common 'Jam Tin'. In the 'hair brush' the explosive and fuse were attached to a wooden handle, whilst a 'Jam Tin', as the name suggests, was literally an empty tin can packed with explosive, and often shrapnel. The method of using either was crude in the extreme; one lit the fuse and hurled it at the enemy. Too short a fuse might lead to a premature detonation, too long a fuse and the grenade might be thrown back.

'Emergency Patterns' of slightly greater sophistication were also produced by the army workshops in France and by manufacturers at home. Amongst the offerings from the army in French bases came the 'Battye' or Bethune grenade, so named after its inventor and place of manufacture respectively. This was a simple cast iron tube, closed at one end, and moulded so as to create an external fragmentation pattern on the casing. From the home factories came bombs like the numbers '6' and '7', colloquially known as 'lemons', small rounded cylinders with friction igniters, and the numbers '8' and '9', which were rather more refined versions of the old 'Jam Tin'. 'Number 12' likewise was a improved version of the 'hairbrush' with the addition of a fragmentation panel which looked rather like a slab of chocolate. None of these bombs was entirely satisfactory and numbers '13' and '14', known as the 'Pitcher' grenades, had a worse reputation than most, earned by either not exploding, or detonating as soon as the friction pull was activated. Perhaps the best known of the Emergency Pattern grenades was the 'Number 15', or ball grenade, a small cast iron sphere looking for all the world like an anarchist's bomb, or a leftover from the Napoleonic wars. It worked tolerably well, but suffered in the wet, even so the soldiery used many of them in 1915 and they were much in evidence at the battle of Loos.

The answer to most of the army's grenade problems turned out to lie with a Belgian army captain and a British marine engineer. The Belgian captain was Leon Roland, who had patented a bomb in England in 1913 which had a fly off handle and a spring igniter, but it was early 1915 before the device had been refined and perfected by William Mills, and introduced to the army. The Mills Bomb, or 'Number 5' as it was placed in the official numbered series, proved powerful, reliable and reasonably inexpensive,

but it was only by placing orders with many diverse industries that production was made even to approximate demand. Finally, with the industrial battle won, about 75 million Mills bombs would be made by 1918.

Mills Bombs came in wooden boxes of 12, which also contained a tin in which were the igniter sets. These were only inserted when the bombs were near the front, by unscrewing the base of the bomb. Once live the throwing procedure was reasonably, though not totally, idiot proof. Holding the bomb in the throwing hand with the fingers or thumb over the lever, the pin was pulled out. The bomb was then thrown. As the grenade left the hand the lever flew off and the spring loaded striker snapped down activating the fuse. Five seconds later the bomb blew up. Detailed practical experiments suggested that anyone

A Royal Engineer demonstrates the correct use of the Rifle Grenade Discharger, No 1 Mark I from the *Description and Instructions for Use* of October 1917. The rifle is held barrel downward, and the blank cartridge touched off by means of the right index finger which launches the grenade. The Service Dress and battle order equipment is also text book: RE shoulder titles are worn, as is Pattern 1908 webbing with haversack on the back and Small Box Respirator on the chest.
D.D.V.

An impression by artist Stanley Wood of Lieutenant W.H.G. Jessup of The Duke of Cornwall's Light Infantry winning the Victoria Cross leading a bombing attack.

PLATE 5.

A splendid photograph taken late in the war showing officers and men of the Grenadier Guards with a selection of grenades and other munitions. The NCOs, (left and right) show an interesting combination of badges having on their right upper arms not only rank chevrons but two cloth grenades, the upper one denoting their status as bombers, the lower being a regimental distinction. Both the NCOs have one wound badge on the lower left sleeve, as does one of the officers, one NCO wears cloth shoulder titles, the other metal. The officers wear Service Dress with plain breast pockets, rank badges on the shoulder straps, forage caps with lace around the peak and shirts of two distinct shades. Both appear to be wearing their swords on their Sam Browne belts. Amongst the weaponry are: far left, (held by the sergeant) the rifle with cup discharger; on the table, two German stick grenades and a distinctive Discus grenade; Hale and Newton rifle grenades; a 'No 19' and a 'No 1' percussion hand grenade; several German Egg hand grenades; a sectioned 'No 36' Mills bomb with cup discharger plate, and front right the finned *Granatenwerfer* projectile. The sergeant (far right) holds a rifle with the ring attachment and rodded 'No 23' Mills.

IWM Q 66186.

standing in the open within ten yards of a Mills explosion was certain to be hit; there was some chance of a hit for those within a 20 yard radius, whilst at 25 yards the chances of a wound were four to one against. At 30 yards the chances were ten to one against, whilst at 35 yards a soldier was almost safe. Almost, because large fragments like the base plug could, and sometimes did, travel much further.

Though the Mills Bomb was highly effective, and by the time of the battle of the Somme had ousted most other less effective types, some new hand thrown bombs were introduced later in the war. Perhaps foremost amongst these was the 'No 34' or 'Egg' bomb, a small, light and handy ovoid of metal, designed to answer a similar bomb used by the Germans, which had a greater range than the heavier types. Also brought in were various forms of phosphorous bomb, intended to have a burning effect, and often gruesomely lethal in the confines of a trench or dugout.

Grenades projected from rifles had been invented several years before the war by a Briton, Frederick Marten Hale, yet at the outbreak of war the whole British army is believed to have been in possession of only a single box. There were several rifle projected models of Hale grenade but most worked on a similar principle: the rifle was loaded with a special blank cartridge and the rod of the rifle bomb was slipped down the barrel. The rifle was then fired to launch the

A wooden grenade launching stand in use in the trenches, c. 1915. Note also the officer in the background wearing a neat woollen cap with pom pom, boots and a short over jacket.

The 'No 34' egg grenade which was developed in the latter part of the war to counter similar small German bombs.

grenade. Any safety measures were deactivated by the shock of launching and travel through the air, and on landing a striker was jolted forwards to hit the detonator and so set off the bomb. Perhaps the best known of the Hale patterns was the 'No. 3' whose safety features included a wind vane which revolved in flight, and so allowed pins to drop free arming the bomb. Failures to detonate, and the expense of production, led inevitably to further research and development and new simplified models. Between 1916 and 1918 alone no less than ten new rifle percussion models would be introduced. These Hale type rodded grenades could have a range of anything up to 300 yards and sometimes bomb firing rifles were used in conjunction with wooden stands, or even clinometer sights, both of which helped the user to judge the correct angle for the rifle at a given range.

Even by 1916, however, the Hale rifle grenades were being overtaken by something more powerful and easier to produce. This new rifle bomb, known as the 'No 23', was nothing more than a Mills bomb with a short rod which was fitted to the SMLE along with a

ring attachment. This ring attachment, which was secured in place by means of the ordinary bayonet, held down the lever of the bomb after the pin had been withdrawn, and allowed the rifle grenadier to fire the Mills without fear of a premature detonation. The ring attachment was reusable many times, and could

Friction brassards which were worn by bombers on the upper part of the arm, principally during 1915, for the ignition of the various types of emergency grenade which were equipped with match type lighters and fuzes. S.B., M.H.

The Vickers ready for action during the battle on Menin Road
Ridge, September 1917. The Highlander on the right of the
picture, with three wound stripes, is wearing a captured
German cap and examining his appearance in a small mirror.
IWM Q 2864.

be carried separately until needed. The range of the
'No 23' was only about 80 yards, yet it had significant
advantages in that it could also be hand thrown, and
was likely in its main essentials to be familiar to
soldiers who were already trained on the old 'No 5'
Mills bomb.

The 'No 23' had apparently been in use for only a
few months before it was realised that both the French
and the German armies were beginning to use rifle
launched bombs which required no rod, and
development was begun of a second generation of rifle
launched Mills bomb. The result was the 'No 36',
which again looked to the casual observer very much
like the original Mills. The main distinction of 'No
36' was in its method of launching when used as a rifle
bomb, since prior to firing it was fitted with a large
circular base plate and was loaded into a cylindrical
Cup Discharger which was fitted to the muzzle of the
rifle by means of claw like levers. General instructions
for the use of the Rifle Grenade Discharger No 1

Mark I were issued in 1917, and by the end of the war
the usual battalion establishment was no less than 96
per battalion with a further ten spares held in reserve.
The 'No 36' cup discharger system offered
considerable advantages since its maximum range was
between 220 and 240 yards, and range alterations
could be carried out by opening and closing a small
vent in the side of the discharger rather than altering
the angle of the rifle. The success of the system may
be judged by the fact that like the Vickers machine
gun it continued in use until the 1960s.

It was inevitable that the many new types of
grenade should bring with them a mass of equipment
which would alter the appearance of a soldiers' kit. As
early as August 1914, Hale rifle grenades were being
ordered with 'Willcock Pattern' carriers. Three basic
designs are known from photographs, all in the form
of a leather oblong, worn as a belt, to which the
grenades were attached by short wide leather straps
fastened by a stud. In one version the carrier had
provision for four grenades, in another there was space
for just three grenades, four launching cartridges, a
small flap top pouch, and a holder for four rope tails
which could be attached to the Hale bombs in place of
the rod so that the bombs could be thrown by hand
instead. Willcock Pattern carriers were probably never

used in any great quantity, and it is unlikely that they were seen much beyond the first year of the war.

Pouches, haversacks and bandoleers for bombs were doubtless all improvised from an early date, but one of the first official descriptions of a carrier appeared in the document *Notes From the Front*, published in May 1915. This was described as a belt which went around the body and was supported by straps over the shoulder and around the waist leaving the wearer with both hands free to fight. It was apparently the precursor of many such devices, for before 1915 was over, at least three other methods of carriage would receive official notice and be promoted to the army as a whole. These were the use of a basket or box with a strap handle; a six pocket haversack each division of which would take either one or two grenades depending on type; and a canvas stick grenade carrier worn on the chest with straps over the shoulders and ties around the waist. Photographic evidence suggests that one or more of these were already official issue by the summer of 1915. It is known that 10,000 two pocket grenade haversacks were ordered from Cooper and company that October, and that a six pocket carrier was ordered from Deyong Limited in December.

This, however, was only a beginning, for by April 1916 several contractors, the most important of which was G.H. Leavy and Company, appear to have been racing with the demand for bomb carriers. Over a quarter of a million items were ordered that month alone. One type of carrier, which appears to have made its debut at about this time, was the so called Belt bag carrier, a canvas bag with a steel hook, closed with a string, which was designed to accommodate four Mills bombs and was hung from the waist belt. Bucket carriers were by now also a common sight, and could take the form of an official issue canvas bucket with a double bottom which was capable of taking anything up to 20 bombs, or could be improvised using sandbags, sometimes stiffened with wire netting, and with a rope handle added. Manuals of 1917 mentioned one further variation on the theme, suggesting the use of the ordinary Pattern 1908 webbing haversack, modified by the simple expedient of punching small holes in the bottom, for the easy carriage of rodded rifle grenades. There were also at least three other patterns of carrier which saw some use on an experimental or limited issue basis: the 'Experimental Workshop' pattern rifle grenade carrier, which was essentially a long cylinder fitted with a sling; the 'R.R.' grenade carrier which held no less than 16 Mills bombs on spring hooks; and the rather dangerous sounding 'Rogers', which was a steel rod

from which six 'No 34' egg grenades dangled.

In what may well have been an administrative tidying up exercise, formal specifications for grenade carriers were issued, or possibly re-issued, during the course of 1918. The specification for the Carrier, Hand Grenades, 'Bucket' type, (Mark I) appeared in May 1918. This stated that bucket carriers were to be of khaki canvas in the form of a seamed sleeve, the bottom of which was to be lined with canvas or linen 'dowlas' material. The carrying handle was to take the form of a two inch wide khaki webbing strap, and the bucket was to be marked internally with contractor and date. In September 1918 was issued the official specification for the 'Carrier, Hand Grenades, with 10 pockets (Mark I)'. This was to be made of khaki drill, and be fitted with ten pockets, arranged in two rows of five, and was to be fastened round the waist with ties. The main supporting strap passed around the neck of the wearer, and was supposed to be able to stand a breaking strain of no less than 300 lb. The specification for the Carrier, Hand Grenades, Waistbelt (Mark I) stated that this device was to be made of hessian with a steel belt hook. If nothing else these specifications gave some clue as to which forms of carrier stood the test of time, and perhaps were most likely to be encountered in the field, since a Routine Order of May 1916 had granted approval to these same three general types.

Artillery, Tanks and Gas

Though space precludes a detailed description of all the many different varieties of artillery and tanks used by British forces in the Great War, no account of the army and its appearance would be complete without at least an outline of the heavier weapons, and the dress of the troops which manned them.

In the 30 years which preceded 1914, artillery equipment had undergone a significant series of changes, indeed in many ways greater advances had been made in the field of artillery than in small arms. At the heart of these advances were the development of new propellants, an increasing ability to manufacture high explosive shells, and increased speed of loading and firing, brought about by fixed charge ammunition combining both shell and propellant in the same unit, and also the use of hydraulic buffers to absorb recoil. The yardstick which set the pace was undoubtedly the French 75 mm field gun, unveiled in 1897, yet even then the full tactical implications of the introduction of the Quick Firer to the battlefield were only imperfectly understood. Artillery in ever greater amounts and increasing calibres would come to dominate the battlefield, slowing down attacks just as effectively as the machine gun, and indeed causing even greater casualties.

The Royal Regiment of Artillery, which traced its ancestry back to the early 18th century, was by 1914 divided into several branches. The most important of these were the Royal Field Artillery (R.F.A.), the Royal Horse Artillery, (R.H.A.) and the Royal Garrison Artillery (R.G.A.). All of these and their 'Territorial' equivalents were wearing Service Dress by the time they appeared in the field, with an approximation of the infantry style for the dismounted services, and mounted breeches and leggings for riders. Brass shoulder titles with the relevant abbreviation distinguished the various types of artillery. Artillery formations never carried colours, regarding the guns themselves as the symbolic heart and rallying point of the unit.

The main duty of the Royal Field Artillery was to provide guns to accompany the infantry divisions. Their basic weapon was the 18 pounder Quick Firer, a gun which was essentially the result of the deliberations of the 'Field Gun Committee' in the wake of the Boer War. It fired a shrapnel shell, weighing 18.5 lb and containing 364 shrapnel balls, to a range of 6,500 yards. Also available to the Field gunners but in smaller numbers, was the 4.5 inch howitzer, a Coventry Ordnance Works design capable of throwing a 35 lb shell 7,300 yards. Anything heavier than this was usually the province of the Royal Garrison Artillery, who, as their name suggested, were responsible for position and siege artillery. In August 1914 the BEF had only two heavy batteries of four guns each attached at Corps level. These heavy batteries were equipped with the 60 pounder, which had a range of 12,300 yards. The only other artillery piece with the army at that time was the 13 pounder, similar to the 18 pounder but lighter and particularly suited to the rapid movements of the Royal Horse Artillery.

Very quickly it was realised that though the Horse and Field artilleries provided competent and often brave support to the infantry, as was exemplified by the V.C. action at Nery, the gunners were woefully deficient in three important areas. The first of these was ammunition, for the issue scales had been drawn up with moderate size intermittent actions in mind – there simply were not enough shells to go round. The result was a shell scandal, and eventually the formation of a Ministry of Munitions to oversee war production. The second shortfall was in heavy guns. The 13 and 18 pounder shrapnel shells were highly efficient against targets in the open, but were of only marginal effectiveness against troops in field fortifications. Lastly, and equally importantly, signalling and communication were ineffective. In mobile war, signal flags, heliographs and dispatch riders were little more useful than their equivalents of the 19th century. In

A long barrelled 6 inch B.L. gun in action. Notice not only the shirt sleeve order of the gunners and their winter ear flap caps, but the men foreground left, one opening the massive charge holders, the other setting the shell fuzes. Daily Mail Battle Pictures, Official Series 5, Number 36.

static trench warfare the field telephones that existed were too few, poorly arranged and prone to cable breaks. Insufficient emphasis pre-war had been paid to predicted fire and fire directed by Forward Observers with the result that too often guns which had a range of several miles were caught within reach of enemy rifles and machine guns.

The first two years of war were spent very much in the rectification of these basic ills. High explosive shells were introduced for the 18 pounder, and heavy guns of many descriptions were brought in to deal with earthworks and barbed wire. Shell production was stepped up, new telephone exchanges were installed, new ranging methods involving sound and flash sighting were brought in, and wireless telegraphy was slowly advanced. Even so it would be late 1916 before all the problems which had been apparent late in 1914 would be thoroughly dealt with. By the time of Neuve Chapelle in March 1915, new equipment had arrived at the front. Amongst this were the elderly 4.7 inch types, veterans of the Boer War fitted with new carriages, 6 inch howitzers, two siege batteries of which arrived just in time to fire in the battle, and 9.2 inch howitzers. Perhaps the most important new weapon, was the 15 inch howitzer. This monster was christened 'Grannie' and it was soon to demonstrate

its effectiveness in inflicting damage against even the deepest of dugouts. Altogether 340 guns were gathered for Neuve Chapelle – it was but a small taste of things to come.

During 1916, shell production climbed from one million seven hundred thousand rounds per month, to more than six million three hundred thousand. By the time of the opening of the battle of the Somme, 1,537 guns had been gathered on this sector of the front to unleash the greatest bombardment of the war so far. Unfortunately, however, mere numbers and length of bombardment were proved to be but a part of the problem, for of the guns used almost two thirds were field guns incapable of penetrating deep dug outs. Long preparations also gave the enemy opportunity to take countermeasures. Few if any of the assaulting infantry therefore walked unopposed into the German position, as the High Command had predicted.

If nothing else the Somme certainly demonstrated how much more work and development lay ahead of the artillery arm. The last two years of war therefore saw new targets set in terms of heavy guns and reliable new fuzes; the development of 'creeping bombardments' and 'fire plans'; and the concentration of fire in rapid, rather than long drawn out shoots. Measurable steps had been taken by the time of Messines and the Third Ypres in 1917, yet progress was slow, and frequently painful. In 1918, the revival of more open warfare brought new challenges, including moving guns forward across shell holed terrain, maintaining control in fluid situations and anti-tank work. On both sides changes not only in infantry weapons and tactics, but in artillery techniques would help to bring about something of a revolution in warfare. Trench mortars proved to be one more important innovation in the new system.

At the outbreak of war the British army had no trench mortars, yet just how desirable a portable and compact weapon with a relatively short range and capable of landing bombs into the enemy trenches would be was soon apparent. First experiments were

less than satisfactory, producing amongst other things a 1.57 inch Vickers trench mortar which could throw a light bomb a reasonable distance, or a heavy bomb to an inadequate range. None of the local improvisations were much more useful, and though many of them were better than nothing some were downright dangerous to their crews. Early 1915 also saw the introduction of a host of mechanically powered trench catapults which were more or less impracticable. The best of these were arguably the Gamage which looked very much like an overgrown version of the schoolboy's catapult, and the West Spring Gun which comprised a huge battery of springs with a throwing arm. This could be moved into position by two men carrying it by means of stretcher-like carrying handles. Both the West and the Gamage were quite widely issued, yet neither was capable of throwing anything much bigger than the ordinary hand grenade.

The first really effective weapon was undoubtedly the 2 inch medium mortar, variously known to the

The author follows in his grandfather's footsteps with a 2 inch Trench Howitzer during the preparation of an exhibition on the battle of the Somme. Note the massive toffee apple projectile and the tubular periscope attachment which would have allowed the crew to see out of the mortar pit. IWM. , M.S.

A Stokes mortar being fired from a covered pit by men of the West Yorkshire Regiment. The corporal on the left wears brass shoulder titles with the wording 'W. YORK'. Similarly visible is a small grenade in blue over his chevrons denoting a trained mortar crewman. Also worn are sacking helmet covers and Small Box Respirators. IWM Q 8461.

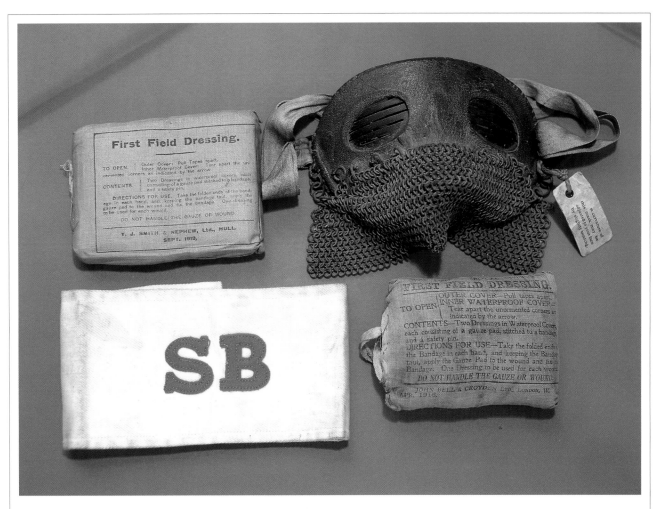

troops as the 'Toffee Apple' or 'Plum Pudding' bomb thrower. These nicknames were remarkably descriptive since the equipment consisted essentially of a wooden bed and a 2 inch diameter tube with elevating and traversing wheels. Into the tube was inserted the metal 'stick' of the 'Toffee Apple', the head of which consisted of a spherical 50 lb high explosive bomb. The projectiles' cartoon confectionery appearance was reinforced by yellow paint with a red stripe. It was capable of a range of about 500 yards, and since it contained 17 lb of explosive was perfectly capable of blowing in dugouts or sections of trench. For short periods it was possible to fire two or even three rounds a minute. By the time of the Somme offensive, three batteries of four of these 2 inch medium mortars were attached to each infantry division. 1916 also saw the authorisation of a blue flaming grenade proficiency badge, worn on the shoulder by both Royal Artillery and infantry trench mortar personnel. In general, Royal Artillery crews tended to man the larger equipments whilst infantry manned the lighter mortars. Painted helmet patches and cloth badges with the letters 'TM' were also known in some formations.

Though production of 3.7 and 4 inch light muzzle loading Trench Howitzers had been commenced at

The armoured face mask of machine gunners and tank crew, pictured here with two different examples of the field dressing and a stretcher bearer's arm band (this last of unknown date). The leather covered tank driver's mask carries a label with the instruction, 'The curvature of this mask may be adjusted to your face by slightly bending.' The field dressings were made by John Bell and Company of Croydon, and T.J. Smith and Nephew of Hull, and dated 1916 and 1918 respectively. M.S., G.C.

the beginning of 1915, neither model proved entirely satisfactory, and their replacement by something rather more revolutionary was begun at the end of the year. This new weapon was the Stokes 3 inch light mortar, a remarkable piece of equipment, which, though it suffered teething problems would eventually become a model for most subsequent light mortar designs of the 20th century. Key to the success of the Stokes was its lightness and simplicity, being effectively a tube closed at one end down which the missile was dropped. A striker ignited the launching charge and blasted the bomb high into the air to explode on impact. For short periods very rapid rates of fire were possible, so fast indeed that several bombs could be airborne simultaneously. For more sustained bombardments a steady rate of five or six rounds per

Tank Corps officers relax around a gramophone. Note that they wear both Machine Gun Corps and other regimental collar badges, coloured 'tallies' on their jacket shoulder straps, and in most instances the white cloth tank badge which was issued in 1917. IWM Q 2897.

minute was perfectly practicable. Eight light mortars made a battery with one per brigade of infantry.

By 1916 therefore the army was concentrating on just three major types of mortar which were effectively light, medium and heavy. The corps level deployed heavy trench mortar was the monstrous 9.45 inch, whose projectiles were known to the troops as 'Flying Pigs'. The heavy mortar was itself essentially a copy of a French design, and was capable, at relatively slow rates of fire, of launching the 150 lb 'Pig' 1,000 yards.

Tanks and Tank Crew Uniform

The tank made its debut on the Somme on 15 September 1916. The Mark I was an immediate, if modest, success, and the lead which Britain established in armoured warfare would remain until the end of the war. The Mark I, which weighed about 28 tons and could manage a gentle walking speed, appeared in both 'male' and 'female' versions. The 'males' were

equipped with two 6 pounder guns and four machine guns, the 'females' with five machine guns. Both had eight man crews. Success led to further orders and to new research and development. The Marks II and III were essentially similar to the original vehicle but were produced in relatively small numbers and after active service at the front were used for training at the tank base at Bovington in Dorset.

The Mark IV, which ultimately became the most common variant in service, entered production in 1917 and began to arrive in France that May. It featured an increased fuel capacity and radius of action; an extra machine gun in the 'female' vehicles, and, at a maximum of half an inch, marginally thicker armour. Though the Mark IV had a maximum range of about 70 miles, poor communication, and lack of suitable battlefield transport for the other arms, ensured that it never became the ultimate 'breakthrough' weapon that some theorists might have wished. Perhaps the closest that such a decisive tank breakthrough came, prior to the final advances of the last autumn of the war, was at Cambrai in November 1917: here no less than 378 Mark IVs were employed in the assault, with a further 54 held in reserve. Even so Cambrai was not planned as as an all out offensive, and counter attacks would soon reclaim most of the ground gained.

The last major models of British tank to be introduced during the Great War took the field in 1918. The Mark V was a traditional rhomboid shape, the main improvements in which were a better gear system and engine, and a further increase in radius of action. More of a radical departure was the 'Whippet' which was in action by the spring of 1918. This was relatively light at 14 tons, was equipped with three machine guns, and, being capable of speeds up to eight miles an hour, was the fastest tank the army possessed. Whippets scored several localised successes in the last six months of the war, including a number in 'open warfare', but the cessation of hostilities precluded further tactical and technological development.

The tanks were originally considered as merely a detachment, but by May 1916 had been renamed as Heavy Section, Machine Gun Corps. From November 1916 the title Heavy Branch was applied, but in July 1917 Royal Warrant confirmed the units independent existence as the Tank Corps. Initially the fighting tanks were fielded in lettered Companies which eventually ran from 'A' to 'F'. Later as numbers increased the Companies were redesignated as Battalions, which ran up to 'L'. Finally the Battalions received numbers, up to 26 by the end of the war.

When the tanks were a part of the Machine Gun Corps, tank crews wore the crossed machine gun cap badges of that unit, but after the formation of the Tank Corps a new badge was authorised. This new badge featured a tank within a laurel wreath, surmounted by an Imperial Crown and the words Tank Corps. A white embroidered tank badge for all those who had passed the tank training course was sanctioned from May 1917, and this was worn on the right upper arm. Shoulder titles apparently varied, but included 'M.G.C' and 'H-M.G.C'. A khaki worsted shoulder slide with the letters 'T.C.' made its appearance at the beginning of 1917, and was apparently intended to replace the existing shoulder titles, but since coloured 'tallies' were being worn on the shoulder strap, Routine Orders directed that this be sewn onto the sleeve, just below the 'point of the shoulder'. Officers were usually seconded from other units and thus it was that collar badges or buttons of other regiments and other minor dress variations were frequently seen amongst tank officers. Some tank battalions also adopted distinguishing marks in addition to the coloured tallies; 4th Battalion for example painted their steel helmets blue to match their shoulder strap distinctions, whilst 8th Battalion took a circular red and dark blue flash for the right side of the helmet. After July 1918, 9th Battalion wore

The lowest form of artillery, a somewhat fanciful Caton Woodville illustration of an early trench catapult.

the badge of French 3rd Division on their left cuff as a memento of successful co-operation.

More importantly tanks also brought with them a new body of specialist clothing. The first garment was the humble 'boiler suit' overall. Originally intended primarily for maintenance duties, but often seen in action, these were at first seen in variety of colours including black, blue and even white. Officers appear to have purchased their own, which again added to the variety. 1917 saw the issue of a tan coloured overall, a one piece garment of cotton with a fly front, small collar, patch pocket on the left breast and a button at each cuff. It was loosely cut so as to allow wearing over the Service Dress, but in practice, due to the excessive heat inside the vehicles which also made shorts popular, it was often worn over underwear and shirt. Sometimes an overall was teamed with gym or rope soled shoes which were less slippery and clumsy in the confines of a tank than the issue studded ammunition boot. Where crew members retained the normal Service Dress this was worn with a minimum of equipment, usually of the leather Pattern 1914, and often incorporating the open topped leather holster

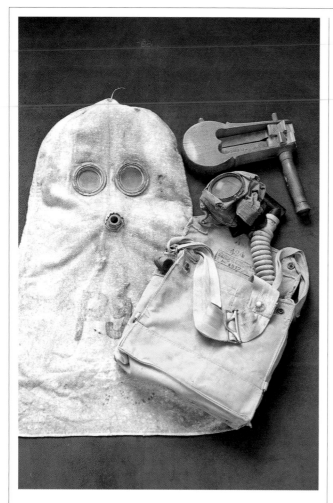

Anti gas equipment 1916-18. Shown here are the grey flannel tube helmet , a Small Box Respirator and a gas warning rattle. The khaki drill bag of the box respirator is marked with the name 'Gillow' of Lancaster, an interesting instance of a furniture company turning its hand to more warlike manufacture. G.C., M.S., Queen's Lancashire Regiment.

also used by the Machine Gun Corps. Puttees were often dispensed with.

The first piece of specialist protective headgear was a brown leather helmet, useful protection against head knocks when being flung around inside a moving tank, but not terribly popular because it was hot and bore an uncomfortable resemblance to the enemy Pickelhaube. It does not seem to have seen much wear after 1916, photographic evidence suggesting that the Service Dress cap and standard steel helmet were preferred. One danger for crews which soon became apparent was the occurrence of bullet 'splash', hot lead and fragments entering through the simple vision slots of the tank. To combat this a face mask was issued. This consisted of a metal plate with armoured eye pieces, faced with dark brown leather and padded inside, from which was suspended a small piece of closely linked mail. White cotton ties secured it to the wearer's head.

Photographs from the latter part of the war suggest that by 1918 a moderately standard garb for other ranks tank crew on active service had evolved. This consisted of the tan overall, boots or shoes without puttees, small box respirator slung around the neck, and the standard steel helmet. In cooler weather, the Service Dress jacket was commonly worn over the overall: on the right upper arm of the jacket appeared the white tank badge, and on the shoulder straps the distinctive 'tallies'. Pistol belts and face masks were added as necessary. It is worth noting that certain armoured car units were crewed by the Royal Navy rather than by the Army which, during the first year of war, were to be seen wearing naval uniform. Later these crews adopted khaki Service Dress, with brown leather equipment and a mixture of RN and army insignia.

Tank Corps shoulder strap 'Tallies' as in use in 1918

1st Battalion	Red
2nd Battalion	Yellow
3rd Battalion	Green
4th Battalion	Light Blue
5th Battalion	Red over Light Blue
6th Battalion	Red over Yellow
7th Battalion	Red over Green
8th Battalion	Red over Dark Blue
9th Battalion	Red over Brown
10th Battalion	Red over White
11th Battalion	Red over Black
12th Battalion	Red over Purple
13th Battalion	Green over Black
14th Battalion	Green over Purple
15th Battalion	Green over Yellow
16th Battalion	Black over Yellow over Black
17th Battalion	Green over White
18th Battalion	Green over Dark Blue
19th Battalion	Red over White over Red
20th Battalion	Red over Yellow over Red
21st Battalion	Red over Black over Red
22nd Battalion	Red over Green over Red
23rd Battalion	Red over Blue over Red
24th Battalion	Green over Yellow over Green
25th Battalion	Green over Black over Green
26th Battalion	Green over White over Green
Tank Carrier Companies	Green over Brown
Gun Carrier Companies	Blue over White over Blue
Central Workshops	Purple
Advanced Workshops	Purple over Yellow over Purple

| Central Stores | Purple over White |
| Salvage Units | Checked, Black and White, or Red and White |

Gas Defence and Attack

Although there had been experiments with poison gas prior to the war, the use of chlorine on the Western Front by the Germans in April 1915 still came as a surprise to the allies. As the war progressed both gas attacks, and gas defence, would make remarkable advances. This process was begun the very day after the first attack when British GHQ instructed that field dressings soaked in bicarbonate of soda should be used as a protection. As nothing more effective was forthcoming the troops and friendly civilians also began immediate production of rudimentary masks. The nuns at Poperinge convent for example were set to work attaching lint strips to tapes, likewise cotton bandoleers and handkerchiefs soaked in water were kept handy by the men in the trenches. Chloroform inhalers were also modified and soaked with lime water, becoming locally known as Bethune respirators after their place of manufacture. At home Lord

Kitchener launched an appeal for cotton wool pads and stockinette masks to be made up by women in Britain. These were intended to be soaked in water, and though well nigh useless, 30,000 were delivered in the first 36 hours of the appeal.

The first effort which was perhaps worthy of the title 'gas mask' was developed by Lieutenant Leslie Barley of 1st Battalion the Cameronians. This again took the form of a pad secured with tapes, but was of cotton waste rather than cotton wool, and was soaked in a solution of sodium hyposulphate and sodium carbonate which would help to render the types of gas then in use chemically harmless. In the first few days, 80,000 such masks were made near the front, and these were teamed with crop sprayers designed to neutralise the gas which entered the trenches. Almost immediately afterwards the War Office sanctioned a similar type to be made at home, using black gauze as a covering. This short lived model of mask became known as the Black Veiling respirator. Useful though they could be it was widely recognised that none of the pad type masks were very efficient and that something better needed to be found.

The next group of masks, or rather helmets since

The dreadful Black Veiling respirator. One of the first official responses to the threat of poison gas. S.J. / Royal Engineers.

Three examples of the special arm band worn by gas troops. Royal Engineers.

Men of 2nd Battalion Argyll and Sutherland Highlanders pictured in the Bois Grenier sector of the trenches in the spring of 1915. They wear pad type gas masks with anti gas goggles: the headgear of three of the men is the 'Balmoral Bonnet'. No badges of any description are visible. IWM Q 48951.

they pulled on right over the top of the head like a balaclava, were developed by Captain Cluny MacPherson, medical officer to the Newfoundland Regiment at British headquarters St. Omer. These chemically impregnated 'hypo' helmets were made up by the Royal Army Clothing Department at Pimlico from grey flannel, and began to arrive at the front in early May 1915. Though a distinct improvement there were problems with the oblong viewing window and the shirt type cloth. Both received modifications and later examples were actually dyed khaki. Although this mask was seen in some numbers it had not been in use long before it was realised that the Germans were developing more virulent forms of gas including phosgene.

Thus it was that further development was carried out: the impregnating chemicals used with masks were changed; the large single window was changed for two eye pieces; and a valve was added through which the soldier breathed out using his mouth. This second major model of helmet gas protection became known as either the 'Phenate' or 'Tube' helmet. It went into general issue, and was carried by the troops in a khaki drill bag with shoulder strap throughout the remainder of 1915. The only significant further modification to the type was another change to the chemicals used to impregnate the mask, thus producing the 'Phenate-Hexamine' helmet. This would see service throughout 1916 and the battle of the Somme. Edmund Blunden, an officer in the Royal Sussex, thought that the flannel helmets were well respected, though mainly because they kept the ears warm. Otherwise they 'smelt odd', and 'breathing in it became sugary, while the goggles seemed inevitably veiled with moisture, highly beneficial in a crisis to one's opponent'.

The final group of respirators used by the British army in the Great War were by all measures the most effective, and had to be since the offensive capabilities of new poison gases were increasing all the time. The development of box respirators, that is gas masks with separate face masks and filter boxes joined by a tube, started as early as the end of 1915 when Boots of Nottingham began production of a granule capable of absorbing poison gas. The first version of the 'box' respirator, issue of which began to the Royal Artillery in 1916, was very bulky and known either as the Large Box Respirator or Harrison's Tower Respirator. This was rapidly succeeded by the much more manageable Small Box Respirator which would become a general issue and see out the war.

The 'S.B.R.' has been acclaimed as the most effective general purpose mask of the period. It consisted of a loosely fitting mask, made by pleating a flat piece of proofed material, with goggles for the eyes. A nose clip ensured that all breathing was via the mouth tube. In the tube was a valve which allowed breathing out, whilst incoming air was sucked up through the bottom of the filter box, which contained the neutralising granules. The mask bag was worn on the chest supporting the box and allowing a reasonable freedom of movement, though mounted men sometimes wore the box bag on the back or side of their bodies minimising the inconvenience of bounce when trotting. Issue of the 'S.B.R.' was completed in early 1917. By the end of the war 13.5 million such masks had been made, and they were also used by other allied powers including the Americans.

Though the most important defensive measure, gas masks were but part of the story of the anti-gas effort. Gloves and linen suits were also used, not normally during attacks but rather by troops operating in areas which had previously been poisoned by mustard gas. Mustard gas was a very nasty compound first used in July 1917, and was a particular problem since it burned and blistered the skin, and depending on weather conditions might persist in the ground for weeks. Animals also received rudimentary protection: horses were being fitted with a small haversack stowed between the cheek pieces of the bridle. When gas struck, the bag was unfolded and fitted like a nose bag. It was not terribly effective but did at least prevent the horse from eating contaminated fodder. For pigeons the protection was equally simple, their baskets being packed inside special impregnated cases.

In terms of reply with gas attacks of their own the British relied first and foremost on the Royal Engineers. As early as June 1915, approval was given for the formation of Special Companies for gas attack, in the same way as other engineer companies were raised for duties such as tunnelling. Members of the Special Companies were picked in the first instance because they had some knowledge of chemicals or chemistry, and were distinguished by the fact that the lowest rank in the unit was that of corporal.

Whilst other nations put more emphasis on the delivery of gas by shells, British tactics more often favoured cylinder release. Shells had the advantage

Irish Guardsmen at gas drill in the Somme area, September 1916. The gear being used is the tube helmet, which is contained in the small khaki drill bag hung around the shoulder when not in use. The men wear small 'I.G.' flashes on the upper arm in lieu of shoulder titles. IWM Q 4232.

that they could be more precisely directed and with a greater element of surprise, but cylinders on the other hand were capable of releasing much larger amounts of gas in greater concentrations. In 1916, Lieutenant W.H. Livens of 'Z' Company sought to combine the advantages of both cylinder and shell in a new device which was to become known as the Livens Projector. This was a short tube, sunk in the ground and electronically fired, in order to send a hefty canister of gas into the enemy line, or just short of it so as to smother the position. They were usually deployed in large batteries so as to achieve maximum effect and surprise. Though first tested with an incendiary bombs, Livens Projectors were soon in use with gas projectiles and proved remarkably effective.

Regiments and Corps

The following list gives the Regiments and Corps as titled (and spelt) in the official *Army List* of July 1914, except where a unit or title post dates the outbreak of war in which case this is noted. They are not in strict order of precedence, but grouped thematically: Guards, Line Infantry, Territorial Force Infantry Regiments, Cavalry, Artillery and Corps. The total number of battalions (or regiments) is given, though it should be noted that in some instances not all battalions were in existence simultaneously. Troops from all theatres and the Home Front are summarised.

The Guards

Title	Total Battalions
Grenadier Guards	5
Coldstream Guards	5
Scots Guards	3
Welsh Guards [raised 1915]	2

Maximum strength achieved by Footguards **49,107**

Line Infantry

The Royal Scots (Lothian Regiment)	34
The Queen's (Royal West Surrey Regiment)	27
The Buffs (East Kent Regiment)	15
The King's Own (Royal Lancaster Regiment)	17
The Northumberland Fusiliers	51
The Royal Warwickshire Regiment	30
The Royal Fusiliers (City of London Regiment)	47
The King's (Liverpool Regiment)	49
The Norfolk Regiment	19
The Lincolnshire Regiment	19
The Devonshire Regiment	29
The Suffolk Regiment	23
Prince Albert's (Somerset Light Infantry)	18
The Prince of Wales's Own (West Yorkshire Regiment)	35
The East Yorkshire Regiment	19
The Bedfordshire Regiment	21
The Leicestershire Regiment	22
The Royal Irish Regiment	10
Alexandra, Princess of Wales's Own (Yorkshire Regiment)	24
The Lancashire Fusiliers	31
The Royal Scots Fusiliers	18
The Cheshire Regiment	38
The Royal Welsh Fusiliers	40
The South Wales Borderers	21
The King's Own Scottish Borderers	14
The Cameronians (Scottish Rifles)	27
The Royal Inniskilling Fusiliers	13
The Gloucestershire Regiment	24
The Worcestershire Regiment	22
The East Lancashire Regiment	17
The East Surrey Regiment	18
The Duke of Cornwall's Light Infantry	15
The Duke of Wellington's (West Riding Regiment)	22
The Border Regiment	16
The Royal Sussex Regiment	26
The Hampshire Regiment	22
The South Staffordshire Regiment	17
The Dorsetshire Regiment	11
The Prince of Wales's Volunteers (South Lancashire Regiment)	21
The Welsh Regiment	35
The Black Watch (Royal Highlanders)	22
The Oxfordshire and Buckinghamshire Light Infantry	18
The Essex Regiment	30
The Sherwood Foresters (Nottinghamshire and Derbyshire Regiment)	33
The Loyal North Lancashire Regiment	21
The Northamptonshire Regiment	13
Princess Charlotte of Wales's (Royal Berkshire Regiment)	16
The Queen's Own (Royal West Kent Regiment)	18
The King's Own (Yorkshire Light Infantry)	24
The King's (Shropshire Light Infantry)	12

The Duke of Cambridge's Own	
(Middlesex Regiment)	49
The King's Royal Rifle Corps	28
The Duke of Edinburgh's (Wiltshire Regiment)	10
The Manchester Regiment	44
The Prince of Wales's	
(North Staffordshire Regiment)	19
The York and Lancaster Regiment	22
The Durham Light Infantry	42
The Highland Light Infantry	33
Seaforth Highlanders	
(Ross-Shire Buffs, The Duke of Albany's)	17
The Gordon Highlanders	23
The Queen's Own Cameron Highlanders	14
The Royal Irish Rifles	21
Princess Victoria's (Royal Irish Fusiliers)	14
The Connaught Rangers	6
Princess Louise's	
(Argyll and Sutherland Highlanders)	26
The Prince of Wales's Leinster Regiment	
(Royal Canadians)	7
The Royal Munster Fusiliers	11
The Royal Dublin Fusiliers	11
The Rifle Brigade (The Prince Consort's Own)	28

Territorial Regiments

Honourable Artillery Company	3
Monmouthshire Regiment	10
The Cambridgeshire Regiment	4
The London Regiment	88
The Hertfordshire Regiment	4
The Herefordshire Regiment	3
Cyclist Battalions	
(Northern, Highland, Kent, and Huntingdonshire)	12

Maximum Infantry Strength Achieved (Line and Territorial) **2,063,688**

Cavalry

The Household Cavalry
1st Life Guards
2nd Life Guards
Royal Horse Guards

The Dragoon Guards
1st (King's) Dragoon Guards
2nd Dragoon Guards (Queen's Bays)
3rd (Prince of Wales's) Dragoon Guards
4th (Royal Irish) Dragoon Guards
5th (Princess Charlotte of Wales's) Dragoon Guards
6th Dragoon Guards (Carabiniers)

7th (Princess Royal's) Dragoon Guards

Cavalry of the Line
1st Royal Dragoons
2nd Dragoons (Scots Greys)
3rd (King's Own) Hussars
4th (Queen's Own) Hussars
5th (Royal Irish) Lancers
6th (Inniskilling) Dragoons
7th (Queens Own) Hussars
8th (King's Royal Irish) Hussars
9th (Queens Royal) Lancers
10th (Prince of Wales's Own Royal) Hussars
11th (Prince Albert's Own) Hussars
12th (Prince of Wales's Royal Lancers)
13th Hussars
14th (King's) Hussars
15th (The King's) Hussars
16th (The Queen's) Lancers
17th (Duke of Cambridge's Own) Lancers
18th (Queen Mary's Own) Hussars
19th (Queen Alexandra's Own) Hussars
20th Hussars
21st (Empress of India's Own) Lancers

The Yeomanry

	Regiments raised
Ayrshire Yeomanry (Earl of Carrick's Own)	3
Bedfordshire Yeomanry	3
Buckinghamshire Yeomanry (Royal Bucks. Hussars)	3
Cheshire (Earl of Chester's)	3
Denbighshire Yeomanry	3
Derbyshire Yeomanry	3
Royal 1st Devon Yeomanry	3
Hampshire Yeomanry (Carabiniers)	3
Hertfordshire Yeomanry	3
Royal East Kent Yeomanry	
(Duke of Connaught's Own)	3
West Kent Yeomanry (Queen's Own)	3
Lanarkshire Yeomanry	3
Lancashire Hussars Yeomanry	3
Duke of Lancaster's Own Yeomanry	3
Leicestershire Yeomanry (Prince Albert's Own)	3
Lincolnshire Yeomanry	3
City of London Yeomanry (Rough Riders)	3
1st County of London Yeomanry	
(Duke of Cambridge's Hussars)	3
2nd County of London Yeomanry	
(Westminster Dragoons)	3
3rd County of London Yeomanry (Sharpshooters)	3
Lothians and Border Horse Yeomanry	3
1st Lovat Scouts Yeomanry	3
2nd Lovat Scouts Yeomanry	3

Montgomeryshire Yeomanry		3
Norfolk Yeomanry (King's Own Royal)		3
Northamptonshire Yeomanry		3
Northumberland Yeomanry (Hussars)		3
Nottinghamshire Yeomanry (Sherwood Rangers)		3
Nottinghamshire Yeomanry (South Nottinghamshire Hussars)		3
Oxfordshire Yeomanry (Queen's Own Oxfordshire Hussars)		3
Pembroke Yeomanry (Castlemartin)		3
Scottish Horse		9
Shropshire Yeomanry		3
North Somerset Yeomanry		3
West Somerset Yeomanry		3
Staffordshire Yeomanry (Queen's Own Royal)		3
Suffolk Yeomanry (The Duke of York's Own Loyal)		3
Surrey Yeomanry (Queen Mary's)		3
Sussex Yeomanry		3
Warwickshire Yeomanry		3
Welsh Horse Yeomanry		3
Westmoreland and Cumberland Yeomanry		3
Royal Wiltshire Yeomanry (Prince of Wales's Own Royal)		3
Worcestershire Yeomanry (The Queen's Own Worcestershire Hussars)		3
Yorkshire Dragoons (Queen's Own)		3
Yorkshire Hussars Yeomanry (Alexandra, Princess of Wales's Own)		3
East Riding of Yorkshire Yeomanry		3

The Reserve and Special Reserve Cavalry

1st Life Guards Reserve Regiment	1
14 (Numbered) Reserve Cavalry Regiments	14
North Irish Horse	2
South Irish Horse	2
King Edward's Horse (The King's Overseas Dominions Regiment)	3

(Many of the Yeomanry regiments were dismounted in 1917 to provide extra battalions for the infantry)

Maximum strength of Household cavalry	**7,618**
Cavalry and Yeomanry	**135,046**

Artillery and Corps

Royal Regiment of Artillery
  (including Royal Horse, Royal Field, Royal Garrison, Territorial equivalents)
  Maximum Strength **548,780**

Corps of Royal Engineers
  (including Signal Service, Electrical, Special

Companies, Railway Staff Corps, and Territorial units)
  Maximum Strength **237,370**

Royal Flying Corps
  (independent 'Royal Air Force' from 1918)
  Maximum Strength **144,078**

Army Service Corps
  ('Royal' from 1918)
  Maximum Strength **314,693**

Army Ordnance Corps
  ('Royal' from 1918)
  Maximum Strength **40,446**

Royal Army Medical Corps
  Maximum Strength **143,984**

Army Veterinary Corps
  ('Royal' from 1918)
  Maximum Strength **29,452**

Army Pay Department
  Maximum Strength **14,549**

Corps of Military Police
  (Independent badged Corps with separate establishment formed post 1918)

Army Chaplains
  Maximum Strength **3,475** (all denominations)
  (styled 'Royal Army Chaplains Department' 1919)

Queen Alexandra's Imperial Military Nursing Service
  Maximum Strength **13,117**

Territorial Force Nursing Service
  Maximum Strength **10,549**

Machine Gun Corps
  (formed 1915–1916)
  Maximum Strength **124,402**

Tank Corps
  (formed as separate entity 1917)
  Maximum Strength **28,299**

Labour Corps
  (Formed 1917)
  Maximum Strength **389,895**

Queen Mary's Army Auxilliary Corps
                (formed 1917 'Q.M.' title granted 1918)
            Maximum Strength **40,850**

Estimated total strength of British Army November
1918, not counting Empire formations   **3,563,466**
Additional Volunteer formations   **248,444**
Prisoners held by enemy countries approx. **150,000**

**Approximate Grand Total British Land Forces
1918   4,000,000**

Basic Unit 'War Establishments' 1914

Cavalry Regiment: HQ & MG Section 8 Officers, 67
                   Other Ranks. 3 Squadrons each of
                   6 Officers and 152 Other Ranks.
                   Each squadron composed of four
                   troops. [N.B. Some units,
                   especially in the Yeomanry, had a
                   four squadron organisation at the
                   outbreak of war. This was rapidly
                   changed to three but in at least
                   one case the resulting three
                   squadrons were lettered A,C,D,
                   rather than the more usual A,B,C]
                   Total 549 all ranks.

Infantry Battalion: HQ and MG Section 6 Officers,
                   93 Other Ranks. Four Companies
                   each of six Officers, and 221
                   Other Ranks. Each company
                   composed of four Platoons, each
                   Platoon of four Sections. [N.B.
                   four company organisation had
                   only been adopted in 1913 with
                   the result that some Territorial
                   units were still changing in 1914.]
                   Total 1007 all ranks.

Artillery Battery Establishments

13pdr Horse   5 Officers, 200 Other Ranks, 6 guns.
18pdr Field   5 Officers, 193 Other Ranks, 6 guns.
4.5 in Howitzer 5 Officers, 192 Other Ranks, 6 guns.
60pdr, Heavy   5 Officers, 163 Other Ranks, 4 guns.
6 in Howitzer   5 Officers, 177 Other Ranks, 4 guns.

Specialist Corps sub units

Royal Engineers
Field Company   6 Officers, 211 Other Ranks.

Divisional
Signal Company 5 Officers, 157 Other Ranks.
Divisional 'Train',
ASC   26 Officers, 402 Other Ranks.
Field Ambulance,
RAMC   10 Officers, 244 Other Ranks.

Establishment of the Complete Infantry Division

Divisional Headquarters	15 officers, 67 other ranks.
3 Infantry Brigades	372 officers, 11,793 other ranks.
HQ Divisional Artillery	4 officers, 18 other ranks.
3 Field Artillery Brigades	69 officers, 2,316 other ranks.
1 Field Artillery (Howitzer) Brig	22 officers, 733 other ranks.
1 Heavy Battery and Am. col	6 officers, 192 other ranks.
1 Divisional Ammunition col	15 officers, 553 other ranks
1 HQ Divisional Engineers	3 officers, 10 other ranks
2 Field Engineer Companies	12 officers, 422 other ranks
1 Signal Company	5 officers, 157 other ranks
1 Cavalry Squadron	6 officers, 153 other ranks
1 Divisional Train	26 officers, 402 other ranks
3 Field Ambulances	30 officers, 672 other ranks
Total riding horses	1,471
Total draught horses	3,350
Total 'heavy' draught horses	644
Total pack horses	127
18 pounder guns	54
4.5 inch howitzers	18
60 pounder guns	4
Machine guns	24
Carts	228
Wagons	648
Motor cars	9
Bicycles	275
Motor cycles	9

Total personnel, 18,073
Total guns, 76

Divisions

The Division as a building block was an important element of the army throughout the war, yet Divisional structures altered markedly between 1914 and 1918. Not only were the number of infantry battalions in each Division reduced from 12 to nine, and units moved from one Division to another, but an increasing number of specialist units were attached at Brigade and Divisional level. For this reason it has been thought apposite to give not an order of battle for the whole BEF at one point in time, but to give typical examples of Divisions at various points during the war. A full description of all Divisions may be found in Major A.F. Becke *Order of Battle of Divisions*, in the *Official History* series published by HMSO in several volumes during the 1930s, and subsequently reprinted. Unit names not immediately apparent from the abbreviated forms given may be checked from the list of *Regiments and Corps* above.

3rd (Regular) Division, August 1914

Commander: Major General HIW Hamilton (killed in action 14.10.14)
Order of Battle for Mons and Le Cateau

7th Brigade
3rd Bn Worcs; 2nd Bn S Lancs; 1st Bn Wilts; 2nd Bn R. Irish Rifles.

8th Brigade
2nd Bn R. Scots; 2nd Bn R. Irish; 4th Bn Middlesex; 1st Bn Gordon H.

9th Brigade
1Bn N. Fus; 4th Bn R. Fus; 1st Bn Lincs; 1st Bn R. Scots Fus.

Mounted Troops
A Sqdn. 15th Hussars; 3rd Cyclist Coy.

Artillery
XXIII Brigade (107, 108, 109 Batteries): XL Brigade (6, 23, 49 Batteries): XLII Brigade (29, 41, 45 Batteries): XXX Howitzer Brigade (128, 129, 130, How. Batteries): 48 Heavy Battery, with their respective ammunition columns.

Also, 56th and 57th Coys. R.E.; 3rd Div. Signal Co; 7th, 8th,9th Field Ambulances; 11th Mobile Vet. Sec; 3rd Div Train.

Guards Division, September 1915
Commander: Major General Earl of Cavan
Order of Battle for Loos

1st Guards Brigade
2nd Bn Gren. Gds; 2nd Bn Colds. Gds; 3rd Bn. Colds. Gds; 1st Bn Irish Gds. 1st Gds Brig. MG Coy.

2nd Guards Brigade
3rd Bn Gren. Gds; 1st Bn Colds, Gds; 1Bn Scots Gds; 2nd Irish Gds. 2nd Gds Brig. MG Coy.

3rd Guards Brigade
1st Bn Colds. Gds; 4th Bn Gren. Gds; 2nd Bn Scots Gds; 1st Bn Welsh Gds. 3rd Gds Brig. MG Coy.

Mounted Troops
Household Cav. Div. Sqdn; Household Cav. Cyclist Coy.

Artillery
LXXIV Brigade (A,B,C,D Batteries): LXXV Brigade (A,B,C,D Batteries): LXXVI Brigade (A,B,C,D, Batteries): LXI Howitzer Brigade (A,B,C,D, How. Batteries) with their respective ammunition columns.

Also, 55th, 75th and 76th Coys R.E.; Gds Div. Signal Coy; 4th Bn Colds Gds (Pioneers); 3rd, 4th, 9th Field Ambulances; 46th Mobile Vet. Sec; Gds Div. Train.

31st (New Army) Division, 1st July 1916
Commander: Major General R. Wanless O'Gowan
Order of Battle for first day of the Somme

92nd Brigade
10th Bn E. Yorks; 11th Bn E. Yorks; 12th Bn E. Yorks; 13th Bn E. Yorks. (Hull 'Pals' Battalions); 92nd Brig. MG Coy; 92nd TM Battery.

93rd Brigade
15th Bn W. Yorks; 16th Bn W. Yorks; 18th Bn W. Yorks; 18th Bn Durham L.I. (1st Leeds, 1st and 2nd Bradford Pals, and 'County of Durham' Battalions); 93rd Brig. MG Coy; 93rd TM Battery.

94th Brigade
11th Bn E. Lancs; 12th Bn York & Lancs; 13th Bn York & Lancs; 14th Bn York and Lancs. (Accrington, Sheffield, and 1st and 2nd Barnsley 'Pals'); 94th Brig. MG Coy; 94th TM Battery.

Artillery
CLXV Brigade (A,B,C,D How. Batteries); CLXIX Brigade (A,B,C,D How. Batteries); CLXX Brigade (A,B,C,D How. Batteries); CLXXI Brigade (A,B,C,D How. Batteries); X 31; Y 31; and Z 31 Medium TM Batteries; V 31 Heavy TM Battery.

Also 210th, 211th and 223rd (Leeds) Coys R.E.; 31st (Leeds) Signal Coy; 12th (Pioneer) Bn K. O. Yorks. L.I.; 93rd, 94th, 95th Field Ambulances; 41st Mobile Vet. Sec.; 31st Div Amm. Col.; 31st Div Train.

12th (Eastern) Division, (New Army), 2nd July 1916
Commander: Major General A.B. Scott
Order of Battle for the Somme

35th Brigade
7th Bn Norf; 7th Bn Suff; 9th Bn Essex; 5th R. Berks; 35th Brig. MG Coy; 35th TM Battery.

36th Brigade
8th Bn R. Fus; 9th Bn R. Fus; 7th Bn R. Sussex; 11th Bn Middlesex.; 36th Brig. MG Coy; 36th TM Battery.

37th Brigade
6th Bn Queen's W. Surrey; 6th Bn Buffs; 7th Bn E. Surrey; 6th Bn Q. O. R. W. Kent; 37th Brig, MG Coy; 37th TM Battery.

Artillery
LXII Brigade (A,B, C, D How. Batteries); LXIII

Brigade (A,B,C,D How. Batteries); LXIV (Brigade A,B,C, Batteries); LXV Brigade (A,B,C,D How. Batteries); X 12, Y 12, Z 12 Medium TM Batteries; V 12 Heavy TM Battery [formed 31.7.16].

Also 69th, 70th, 87th Coys. R.E.; 12th Signal Coy; 12th (Pioneer) Bn Northamptons.; 36th, 37th, 38th Field Ambulances; 23rd Mobile Vet Sec; 12th Div Amm. Col. ; 12th Div Train.

1st Cavalry Division, September 1916
Commander: Major General R.L. Mullens
Order of Battle for Flers-Courcelette, when serving in reserve to XIV Corps, Fourth Army on the Somme

1st Cavalry Brigade
2nd Dragoon Gds (Queen's Bays); 5th Dragoon Gds; 11th Hussars. I Battery R.H.A.; 1st Cav Brig. MG Sqdn.; 1st Signal Troop.

2nd Cavalry Brigade
4th Dragoon Gds; 9th R. Lancers; 18th Hussars; H Battery R.H.A.; 2nd Cav Brig. MG Sqdn.; 2nd Signal Troop.

9th Cavalry Brigade
15th Hussars; 19th Hussars; 1st Bedfordshire Yeomanry. Y Battery R.H.A.; 9th Cav Brig. MG Sqdn.; 9th Signal Troop.

Light Armoured Cars
8 Battery Motor Machine Gun Corps.

Also 1st Field Sqdn. R.E.; 1st Signal Squadron; 1st, 3rd, 9th, cav. Field Ambulances; 1st , 10th, 39th Mobiles Vet Secs; 27th (HT) Coy (ASC); 57th,58th (MT) Coys ASC; 572 Aux Horse Coy; Amm. Park 45 (MT) Coy. {NB the support services here noted are either horsed or 'Motor Transport' to match cavalry status of Division.}

20th (Light) Division, (New Army), August 1917
Commander: Major General W. Douglas Smith
Order of Battle for Battles of Langemarck, Menin Road Ridge and Polygon Wood; Third Ypres

59th Brigade
10th Bn King's R.R.C.; 11th Bn King's R.R.C.; 10th Bn Rifle Brig.; 11th Bn Rifle Brig; 59th Brig. MG Coy; 59th TM Battery.

60th Brigade
6th Bn Ox & Bucks. L.I.; 6th Bn King's Shrops. L.I.;

12th Bn King's R.R.C.; 12th Bn Rifle Brig; 60th Brig. MG. Coy.;60th TM Battery.

61st Brigade
12th Bn King's (Liverpool); 7th Bn Somerset L.I.; 7th Bn D.O. Cornwall's L.I.; 7th King's O. Yorks. L.I.; 61st MG Coy.; 61st TM Battery.

Artillery
XCI Brigade (A,B,C,D How. Batteries); XCII (A,B,C, D, How. Batteries); X 20, Y 20, Z 20 Medium TM Batteries; V 20 Heavy TM Battery.

Also 83rd, 84th, 96th Coys R.E.; 20th Signal Coy.; 11th (Pioneer) Bn Durham L.I; 217th MG Coy; 60th, 61st, 62nd, Field Ambulances; 32nd Mobile Vet Sec; 221st Div Employment Coy; 20th Div Amm. Col; 20th Div Train.

48th (South Midland) Divison, (Territorial Force), August 1917

Commander: Major General R. Fanshaw
Order of Battle for Battles of Langemarck, Polygon Wood, Broodseinde and Poelcappelle; Third Ypres

143rd Brigade
5th Bn R. Warwicks.; 6th Bn R. Warwicks.; 7th Bn R. Warwicks.; 8th Bn R. Warwicks; 143rd MG Coy.;143rd TM Battery.

144th Brigade
4th Bn Gloucs.; 6th Bn Glous.; 7th Bn Worcs.; 8th Bn Worcs; 144th MG Coy.; 144th TM Battery.

145th Brigade
5th Bn Gloucs.; 4th Ox & Bucks. L.I.; 1st Bucks. Bn Ox & Bucks. L.I.; 4th Bn R. Berks; 145th MG Coy; 145th TM Battery.

Artillery
CCXL Brigade (A,B,C,D How. Batteries); CCXLI Brigade (A,B,C,D How Batteries); X 48, Y48, Z 48 Medium TM Batteries; V 48 Heavy TM Battery.

Also 474th, 475th, 477th (S. Midland) Coys R.E.; 48th (S. Midland) Signal Coy; 251st MG Coy; 1st , 2nd, 3rd, (S.Midland) Field Ambulances; 1st (S. Midland) Mobile Vet Sec.; 242nd Div Employment Coy; 48th Div Amm. Col; 48th Div Train.

16th (Irish) Division, (New Army), March 1918

Commander: Major General Sir C.P.A. Hull
Order of Battle for Battles of St. Quentin and

Rosieres: 'Kaiserschlacht' German offensive

47th Brigade
6th Bn Connaught Rang.; 2nd Bn Leinsters,; 1st Bn R. Munster Fus.; 47th TM Battery.

48th Brigade
2nd Bn R. Munster Fus.; 1st R. Dublin Fus.; 2nd R. Dublin Fus.; 48th TM Battery.

49th Brigade
2nd Bn R. Irish; 7th (S. Irish Horse) Bn R. Irish; 7/8th Bn R. Inniskilling Fus.; 49th TM Battery.

Artillery
CLXXVII Brigade (A,B,C,D How. Batteries); CLXXX (A,B,C,D How. Batteries); X 16, Y 16, Medium TM Batteries.

Also 155th, 156th, 157th Coys R.E.; 16th Signal Coy; 11th (Pioneer) Bn Hants; 16th Bn MG Corps; 111th, 112nd, 113th Field Ambulances; 47th Mobile Vet Sec.; 217th Div Employment Coy; 16th Div Amm. Col; 16th Div Train.

55th (West Lancashire) Division, (Territorial Force) August 1918

Commander: Major General H.S. Jeudwine
Order of Battle during final Advances

164th Brigade
4th Bn King's O. (R. Lancaster); 2/5th Bn Lancs. Fus; 4th Bn Loyal N. Lancs.; 164th TM Battery.

165th Brigade
5th Bn King's (Liverpool); 6th Bn King's (Liverpool); 7th Bn King's (Liverpool); 165th TM Battery.

166th Brigade
5th Bn King's O. (R. Lancaster); 10th King's (Liverpool); 5th Bn S. Lancs.; 166th TM Battery.

Artillery
CCLXXV Brigade (A,B,C,D How Batteries); CCLXXVI Brigade (A,B,C,D How. Batteries); X 55, Y 55 Medium TM Batteries.

Also 419th, 422nd, 423rd, Coys R.E.; 55th Signal Coy; 4 (Pioneer) Bn S. Lancs; 55 Bn MG Corps; 3rd (W. Lancs.), 2/1st (W. Lancs), 2/1st (Wessex) Field Ambulances; 1st W. Lancs Mobile Vet Sec.; 246th Div Employment Coy; 55th Div Amm. Col; 55th Div Train.

Bibliography

Blunden, E., *Undertones of War*, 1928, reprinted Harmondsworth, 1982.

Carman, W.Y., *British Uniform From Contemporary Pictures*, Feltham, 1968.

Chappell, M., *British Infantry Equipments, 1908-1980*, London, 1980.

Chappell, M., *British Battle Insignia, 1914-1918*, London, 1986.

Dawnay, N.P., *The Badges of Warrant and Non-Commissioned Rank in the British Army*, Society for Army Historical Research, London, 1949.

Dean, B., *Helmets and Body Armour in Modern Warfare*, New Haven, CT, 1930.

Dolden, A.S., *Cannon Fodder*, Poole, 1980.

Dunn, J.C., *The War The Infantry Knew*, new edition, London, 1987.

Dunstan, S., *Flak Jackets*, London, 1984.

Edmonds, J.E., (ed), *History of the Great War Based on Official Documents*, Many vols. London, 1922-44.

Edwards D., and Langley, D. *British Army Proficiency Badges*, Nottingham, 1984.

Fisch, R., *Field Equipment of the Infantry, 1914-1945*, Sykesville, MD, 1989.

Fosten, D.S.V., (et al) *The British Army, 1914-1918*, London, 1978.

Frederick, J.B.M., *Lineage Book of British Land Forces*, Wakefield, 1984.

General Staff, *Notes on Protection Against Poisonous Gases*, May, 1915.
Instructions for the Use of Box Respirators, March, 1916.
Some Notes on Lewis Guns and Machine Guns, September, 1916.
Extracts From Routine Orders, January, 1917.
Notes on Inventions and New Stores, 3 Vols. April-October, 1917.
Notes For Infantry Officers on Trench Warfare, 1917.
Instructions For Yukon Pack Use, November, 1917.

Glover, M., (ed) *The Fateful Battle Line: the Great War Journals and Sketches of Captain Henry Ogle, M.C.*, London, 1993.

Hammerton, J.A., *The War Illustrated*, 9 Vols., London, 1914-19.

Hitchcock, 'F.C., *Stand To', A Diary of the Trenches*, London, 1937.

James, E.A., *British Regiments, 1914-1918*, London, 1978.

Joslin, E.C., (et al) *British Battles and Medals*, London, 1988.

A lance corporal of 4th (Territorial) Battalion the Seaforth Highlanders on gas sentry duty at Wancourt, October 1917. Strips of light blue cloth high on the shoulder indicate that this man is in the second unit of 154th Brigade, but no divisional sign for 51st (Highland) Division is displayed. The kilt, often obscured by a khaki kilt apron, is of Mackenzie tartan, the equipment is leather Pattern 1914. The strange object on the post is a Strombos horn, to be sounded in the event of gas attack. IWM Q 6132.

Men of the York and Lancaster regiment pictured near Roclincourt ready to set out on a patrol, 12 January 1918. They wear a variety of robes and crawling suits: hoods are worn, some with cut outs over the ears so not as to impede hearing. A couple of the men wear leggings held tight with exterior straps. IWM Q 23580.

Kipling, A.L., and King, H.L., *Head-Dress Badges of the British Army*, Vol. 1, London, 1978.

Linaker, D., & Dine, G., *Cavalry Warrant Officers' and Non- Commissioned Officers' Arm Badges*, Military Historical Society, London, 1997.

Military Illustrated Magazine, numerous articles, London, 1986, continuing.

Ministry of Munitions, *History of the Ministry of Munitions*, 12 vols, London, 1920.

Mollo, A., and Turner, P., *Army Uniforms of World War I*, Poole, 1977.

Munitions Design Committee, *Trench Warfare Section: Minutes*, London, 1915-18.

Ogilby Trust, *Uniforms of the British Yeomanry Force*, many vols., Aldershot, 1980s and 1990s.

Pegler, M., *British Tommy, 1914-1918*, London, 1996.

Purves, A.A., *The Medals, Decorations, and Orders of the Great War*, Polstead, 1989.

Skennerton, I., *The British Service Lee*, Margate, Australia, 1982.

Skennerton, I., *The British Sniper*, Margate, Australia, 1984.

War Office, *List of Changes in War Material* , London, monthly, 1860 onwards.

The Pattern 1908 Web Equipment, London, 1913.

Regulations for the Clothing of the Army, London, 1914.

Statistics of the Military Effort of the British Empire, 1914-1920, London, 1922.

Dress Regulations For the Army, London, 1911.

Westlake, R.A., *Collecting Metal Shoulder Titles*, London, 1980.

British Territorial Units, 1914-1918, London, 1991.

Wheeler-Holohan, V., *Divisional and Other Signs*, London, 1920.

White, A.S., *A Bibliography of Regimental Histories of the British Army*, new edition, Dallington, 1992.

Wilkinson-Latham, R. and C., *Home Service Helmet, 1878-1914*, London, not dated.

Williamson, H., *A Dictionary of Great War Abbreviations*, Harwich, 1986.

Windrow M., and G. Embleton, *Tank and AFV Crew Uniforms Since 1916*, Cambridge, 1979.

World War One Directory

Museums in the UK

Despite recent cutbacks, associated with the defence review *Options for Change*, the United Kingdom can still boast a remarkable diversity of military museums, many, if not most, of which have something to offer the student of First World War British uniform and equipment. What follows cannot be a compendium of all, but those who wish an exhaustive listing should consult Terence and Shirley Wise, *Guide to Military Museums* (8th revised edition, Doncaster, 1994).

The ultimate collection of Great War material in Britain is undoubtedly that at the Imperial War Museum, Lambeth Road, London, SE1 6HZ (telephone 0171-416 5000). In the early 1990s, the First World War galleries underwent an impressive and expensive refit: at the time of writing they include not only a substantial trench reconstruction but a remarkable array of uniform and equipment ranging from Haig's own Service Dress to trench mortars, snipers' garb, sealed patterns, and a thousand other delights for the ethusiast. One should also bear in mind that the museum's worth does not rest solely its exhibitions; like an iceberg much lies beneath the surface. Many real treasures are to be found (by appointment) in the vast photograph collection housed in a nearby annex, and in the library, or between the pages of the museum's *Review*. The museum shop contains both relevant new books and some reprints of contemporary works. The Imperial War Museum outstation at Duxford Airfield, Duxford, Cambridgeshire (telephone 01223- 83500) is also worth a visit, though the emphsis here is on artillery and larger exhibits. Current news is that an Imperial War Museum branch is planned for the Manchester area, though its content is as yet unknown.

Not as extensive, nor as well visited, but containing a significant collection of First World War uniform, and artefacts is the National Army Museum, in Royal Hospital Road, Chelsea, SW3 4HT (telephone 0171-730 0717). This has a reading room and a photograph collection, both of which may be accessed by appointment. Whilst in central London it is worth noting that the Guards Museum is at Wellington Barracks, Birdcage Walk, London, SW1E 6HQ; and that the Royal Fusiliers have their museum within the Tower of London. Several Territorial units have small collections nearby, though these often require prior arrangements to view (details to be found in, *Guide to Military Museums*).

Also in the London vicinity are the twin museums of the Royal Artillery at Woolwich: the Rotunda contains the guns themselves, whilst just across the common at the Old Royal Military Academy, Red Lion Lane, SE18 4DN is the Regimental Museum proper (telephone 0181–781 5628, ext 3128). Those able to linger in the Kent area may also find much to interest them at the Royal Engineers Museum, Brompton Barracks, Chatham, Kent, ME4 4UG (telephone 01634–406397), at the Buffs Regimental Museum at 18 The High Street, Canterbury, CT1 2JE (telephone 01227–452747), and at Dover Castle where the various regiments which have now gone to make up the Princess of Wales's Royal Regiment and the Queen's Royal Regiment have a museum. At Chelmsford in Essex can be found the collections of the Essex Regiment Museum, Moulsham Street, Chelmsford, Essex, CM2 9AQ (telephone 01254–260614).

The south and south west have many notable collections. Those which may be especially recommended for their Great War artefacts must begin with the awe inspiring Tank Museum at Bovington, Dorset, BH20 6JG (telephone 01929–403329). Less well known, but well endowed with First World War memorabilia, are the Duke of Cornwall's Light Infantry Museum in the Keep at Bodmin (telephone 01208–72810); the recently refurbished Military Museum of Devon and Dorset on

Bridport Road, Dorchester, Dorset, DT1 1RN (telephone 01305–264066); and the veritable complex of Regimental Museums in the Winchester area, several of which have 'Light' infantry connections and are within Peninsular Barracks, Romsey Road, Winchester, SO23 8TS (telephone 01962–864176). Aldershot will likewise absorb a whole day, where one might do worse than begin with the Aldershot Military Museum, Queen's Avenue, Aldershot, Hampshire, GU 11 2LG (telephone 01252–314598) and then explore the various Corps museums.

In the midland area, Warwick boasts no less than three Regimental collections, the largest of which is that of the Royal Warwickshire Regiment, at St. John's House, Warwick, CV 34 4NF (telephone 01926–491635). Just outside Lichfield is the Museum of the Staffordshire Regiment, at Whittington Barracks, Staffordshire, WS14 9PY (telephone 0121–3113225). Gloucester boasts a particularly stylish development in the shape of the Regiments of Gloucestershire Museum, which is located on the old dock, within walking distance of several non-military museums (telephone 01452–522682). The north Midlands has a number of relevant collections including the museum of the 9th/12th Royal Lancer's, within Derby City Museum, and that of the Sherwood Forester's in Nottingham Castle. Out on a limb geographically, but modern in terms of display, is the Royal Norfolk's at the Shirehall, Norwich (telephone 01603–223649).

In the north west, the two largest collections are those of Chester, in the Cheshire Military Museum, The Castle, Chester, CH1 2DN (telephone 01244–327617), and that housed within the Museum of Lancashire, on Stanley St. Preston, PR1 4YP. This includes the complete collections of the 14th/20th King's Hussars and the Duke of Lancaster's Own Yeomanry, as well as a selection of material on the North, South, and East Lancashire Regiments and a trench reconstruction (telephone 01772-264075); further material is to be found at Fulwood Barracks, Preston, and within Blackburn Museum. Also worthy of note are the Border Regiment display in Carlisle Castle; the Manchester's at Ashton-Under-Lyne; and the King's Own at Lancaster within the City Museum. The Lancashire Fusiliers are an extremely distinguished regiment in a less than easy to find location at Wellington Barracks, Bury, Lancashire, (telephone 0161–7642208). The King's Liverpools also have an interesting collection, residing within National Museums and Galleries on Merseyside, though at the time of writing this was undergoing redisplay.

Yorkshire and the North East are arguably less well represented, but even so there are a number of museums having material of First World War interest. Particularly worthwhile are the Green Howards at Trinity Church Square, Richmond, North Yorkshire (telephone 01748–822133); the York and Lancasters at the Central Library and Arts Centre, Walker Place, Rotherham, South Yorkshire, S65 1JH (telephone 01709–382121, ext 3625); and the Durham Light Infantry museum which is at Akyley Heads, Durham City, DH1 5TU (telephone 0191–3842214). York itself has several military museums containing Great War objects, with both the Prince of Wales' Own and the 4th/7th Royal Dragoon Guards on Tower Street, York, YO1 SB1 (telephone 01904–642038, and 642036 repectively), very handy for the Castle Museum and other attractions. Lincoln's military collections, which include a Mark IV tank, form a part of the Museum of Lincolnshire Life, at the Old Barracks, Burton Road, Lincoln, LN1 3LY (telephone 01522–528448).

The most significant concentration of Great War objects in Scotland lie within the walls of Edinburgh Castle, in the Scottish United Services Museum and its satellites. Two regiments particularly well represented are the Royal Scots and the Royal Scots Dragoon Guards, but there is also a library and other facilities (telephone 0131–2257534, ext 400). The museum of the Royal Highland Fusiliers is at 518 Sauchiehall Street, Glasgow, G2 3LW (telephone 0141-3320961), whilst the Queen's Own Highlanders are at Fort George (telephone 01463- 224380) and the Argyll and Sutherland Highlanders are within Stirling Castle, Stirling, FK8 1EH (telephone 01768-475165). Balhousie Castle, Perth, PH15HS, is home to the collection of the Black Watch (telephone 01738-21281, ext 8530).

Cardiff Castle is home to a number of Welsh regimental collections, including that of the Royal Regiment of Wales (telephone 01222–229367). Perhaps better known to holiday makers and readers of regimental histories are the Royal Welch Fusiliers at Caernarfon Castle, Gwynedd (telephone 01286–673362), and the South Wales Borderers at the Barracks, Brecon, Powys, LD3 7EB (telephone 01874–613310).

Those seeking information on individual soldiers rather than on units, equipment, and campaigns should note that many regimental museums do not hold personal service papers, which, where they survive, are with either the Army Records Centre, or the Public Records Office. Some regimental museums do hold unit War Diaries, but again the fullest set is lodged with the Public Records Office.

Touring the Battlefields

Though it is perfectly possible to see the Western Front with the aid of nothing more complex than a bicycle and a copy of Rose Coombs' book, *Before Endeavours Fade,* those who wish for guidance and a more comfortable trip may be interested in consulting a company which specialises in battlefield tours. Perhaps the best known is Holt's Tours, at 15 Market St, Sandwich, Kent, CT13 9DA (telephone 01304–612248), but there are now many alternatives including Battlefield Tours of Birmingham (telephone 0121–459 9008), and Milestone Tours of Nottingham (telephone 0115–943 6212). There is every possibility that your guide will be a retired military man, an impecuneous author or a museum curator. The really adventurous travellers are now seeking out Great War sites further afield in Africa, Palestine and Gallipoli, and with this last in mind the Galliopli Association at 9 Garnet Court, Marlow, Bucks, SL 7 2AN, is a useful point of contact.

Once the Western Front traveller has disembarked there are numerous monuments, preserved trench sites, cemeteries and local museums if you know where to look. If you are seeking a particular grave or memorial, prior contact with Commonwealth

Dismounted tank crew man a Lewis gun post during the enemy offensive on the river Lys, April 1918. Both men wear Service Dress with a small white embroidered tank on the right shoulder, and parts of the Pattern 1914 leather equipment. The holster and pistol with lanyard is clearly visible on the man nearest the camera. IWM Q 6528.

Wargraves at 2 Marlow Rd, Maidenhead, Berks, SL6 7DX (telephone 01628-34221) is invaluable; in France their office is at Rue Angèle Richard, 62217, Beaurains, Nr Arras (telephone 21 71 03 24). Useful orientation is provided not only by the relevant Michelin map for the area of interest, but by Holt's maps of Ypres and the Somme. Fine detail of trench lines and villages as they were during the war can be filled in by consultation of P. Chasseaud's book of trench maps, *Topography of Armageddon* (Lewes, 1991). Around Ypres in Belgium the 'must see' list should include the Salient Museum by the famous Cloth Hall and the Menin Gate. Within easy reach of the town are the vast Tyne Cot British Cemetery, the German cemetery at Langemarck, and the preserved sections of battlefield at Hill 60 and Sanctuary Wood.

Though most of its connections are Canadian rather than British, Vimy Ridge provides one of the most rewarding experiences for the battlefield pilgrim.

Here there are significant sections of preserved trench, and Canadian students spend summer vacations guiding the curious around Grange Tunnel which even yet contains twists of rusting metalwork and evidence of the handiwork of British, Australian and Canadian Engineers. Snipers' loops and mine craters are also to be seen.

Arras is not only a useful starting point for the exploration of the northern Somme battlefields, but has a remarkable system of underground caves which served as the British headquarters. Amiens is better placed for the exploration of the scenes of slaughter on 1 July 1916, since Ovillers, Thiepval, Pozieres and Montauban are no more than a few kilometres away. Particularly special are the Sheffield Memorial Park near Serre, and the remarkable Newfoundland Memorial Park with its significant stretch of preserved trenches, three cemeteries and Caribou statue. Few things in France can be as evocative as the huge hole of Lochnagar Crater, made by 60,000 lb of British explosives. On the subject of which it should go without saying that the munitions, which are found even today, can still be dangerous if tampered with. The present writer has corresponded with a Belgian Army Ordnance Technician, trained in disposal, who succeeded in injuring himself very seriously.

Book Suppliers

There is much to be said for the inter-library loan system, whereby most books in Britain can be had for 50 pence, but if you must possess your own library of books on the Great War two postal suppliers seem to lead the field in terms of quality knowledgeable service. These are Ray Westlake Military Books of 53 Claremont, Malpas, Newport, Gwent, NP9 6PL (telephone 01633–854135), and Ken Trotman of Unit 11, 135 Ditton Walk, Cambridge, CB5 8PY (telephone 01223-211030). Many others are well worth trying for that ellusive volume, as for example Chelifer Books of Todd Close, Curthwaite, Wigton, Cumbria, CA7 8BE (telephone 01228–711388); Athena Books of 34 Imperial Cresent, Town Moor, Doncaster, South Yorkshire, DN2 5BU (telephone 01302–322913); the Military Bookworm at P.O. Box 235, London, SE23 1NS; or Books International of 16 Camp Road, Farnborough, Hampshire, GU14 6EW (telephone 01252-375089).

Re-enactment Societies, Modelling and Wargaming

For many years the Great War was viewed as a not terribly satisfying subject for any of the above, being widely imagined as one endless slaughter which did not involve any idea of progress or tactics. Fortunately perhaps the last 30 years of research, and the passage of time itself, have served to bring the Great War out of the realms of questionable taste and into mainstream interest. As far as modelling and wargaming are concerned there are now quite a few manufacturers and suppliers. Amongst those which spring to mind are *Irregular Minatures* of 30 Apollo St, Heslington Rd, York, YO1 5AP; *The Guardroom*, 38 West St., Dunstable, Bedfordshire, LU6 ITA; *'IT' Figures*, 193 St. Margaret's Rd, Lowestoft, Suffolk, NR32 4HN; *Britannia Miniatures*, 33 St. Mary's Rd, Halton Village, Runcorn, Cheshire, WA7 2BJ; and *Tabletop Games* of 29 Beresford Ave, Skegness, Lincolnshire, PE25 3JF. Many more will be speedily identified by consulting publications such as *Wargames Illustrated*, *Minature Wargames*, *Windrow and Greene's Militaria Directory* or *Military Modelling*.

The main living history society within the UK is undoubtedly *The Great War Society*. Their points of contact include their chairman, R.G. Carefoot, 18 Risedale Drive, Longridge, Nr Preston, Lancs, PR3 3SB and in the south, T. Hill, 2 Tintagel Court, Longthorpe, Peterborough, PE3 6SP. In the United States of America an extremely useful method of getting in touch with re-enactment is through the *Listening Post* newsletter, care of P. Carson, 4630 Campus Avenue, San Diego, CA 92116. Also on the west coast of the US is the *Black Watch* regiment re-enactment group which may be contacted via R. Lunde, 10198 Dennison Ave, Cupertino, CA 95014. Though not a re-enactment society, the *Western Front Association* is extremely useful in terms of research, information concerning visits to the battlefields, and getting to meet like-minded individuals. Two points of contact are their information officer, R. Clifton of 6 Clarendon Rd, Cambridge CB2 2BH, and their membership secretary, P. Hanson, 17 Aldrin Way, Cannon Park, Coventry, W. Midlands, CV4 7DP.

Index

Acknowledgements

Numerous individuals and institutions have been kind enough to provide information and assistance without which this book could have been difficult, if not impossible. I apologise in advance to any inadvertently omitted, but I would especially like to thank the following from the museum world: David Penn, Diana Condell, Mike Hibberd, Hilary Roberts and Paul Cornish of the Imperial War Museum; Dr. Linda Washington of the National Army Museum; Martin Pegler of the Royal Armouries; Ian Hook, Essex Regiment Museum; Simon Davies, Northamptonshire Regiments; Angela Kelsall, 9th/12th Royal Lancers Museum, Derby; Major David Evans, Liverpool Scottish; Colonel John Downham, Major Mike Glover and Major Tony Maher of the Queen's Lancashire Regiment; Major 'Bill' Williams 14th/20th King's Hussars (and latterly King's Royal Hussars); Major John McQ. Hallam, Lancashire Fusiliers Museum; Nicola Frost, Manchester Regiment Museum; Allan Carswell, Scottish United Services Museum; Brigadier Ken Timbers, Royal Artillery Institution; Peter Donnelly, Lancaster City Museum; Stuart Eastwood, Border Regiment Museum, and last, but by no means least Simon Jones, formerly of the Royal Engineers Museum, but latterly of the King's Liverpool Regiment collection at National Museums and Galleries on Merseyside.

The majority of the photographs are from private collections, but where examples have been used from national or local museums or archives, these are individually acknowledged. Regarding assistance with the illustrations, and with readings of parts of the text, I should also like to thank Ray Westlake, military bookseller and researcher extraordinary; Geoff Carefoot, Chairman, Great War Society; badge expert Hugh King; and photographer and 'right hand man' of amazing patience, Mike Seed.